# MY PLACE AMONG FISH

## MISADVENTURES ON THE RIVER

*For ribbons + two
join within.*

*K*

## KRIS MILLGATE

Published by Tight Line Media, Idaho Falls, Idaho
www.tightlinemedia.com

Editor: Avalon Radys
Cover: Tim Barber, Dissect Designs
Interior: Kevin G. Summers

ISBN:  978-1-7371108-0-4
e-ISBN: 978-1-7371108-1-1
LCCN: 2021908106

First edition

Printed in Canada with support from Teton Toyota

Dedicated to my real mom. She didn't talk to me after publication of my first book, *My Place Among Men*, but we closed wounds just in time for her to be the first person to know I had another book in me . . . and more stitches.

# CONTENTS

# NOTE FROM THE AUTHOR

FOLLOW SALMON MIGRATION eight hundred fifty miles from the ocean to Idaho. Impossible. Do it during a global pandemic. More impossible. What does it take to pull off the unbelievable during a catastrophic moment in human history? Somehow, I found the answer, but it took more out of me than I'd anticipated.

What happened in front of the camera appears in the *film Ocean to Idaho*. What happened behind the camera will be revealed in this book.

This is the back story. My back story.

# PROLOGUE:

## Tubs

IF YOU'RE THINKING my favorite place is outside, you're right. Especially by water, but that's when I want to do something. Right now I want to do nothing, so I'm in my favorite do-nothing place. My do-nothing place also has water, but it isn't outside. To do nothing, I go inside, sometimes with lights off, so I see nothing too. If I need to see—like to eat a plate of pickles, crackers, cheese, and olives—I turn on the closet light, but not the bathroom light. It's too direct, too much of something when I'm trying to do nothing. I do a lot of nothing in the tub, but that always sparks something.

For me, all great ideas surface in the best baths. It's where I do my most productive thinking. That's why I negotiate hard for baths instead of showers, even when I can only have half-baths. The fluid swirl of tub is more satisfying than the pelting drops of shower. I normally don't have to negotiate my tub time, but yet again, these are not normal times.

If you read my first memoir, you might have picked up on the fact that my brain doesn't go into book-mode unless I'm wallowing in unexpected discomfort of the extreme sort, like I was when I wrote *My Place Among Men*. That book was born out of the sedentary restlessness of an outdoor journalist with a leg shattered in three places. I'd told myself I wouldn't write another book if it meant I had to break another leg—after all, who wants to go through that painstaking process twice? Fortunately, I didn't break another leg. I lost a body part instead. And all because of a fish. I'll explain later, but first, the bath/half-bath battle.

Doctors say, "Shower okay, so the stitch will stay." I say, "Baths okay, if the stitch is out of the way." They agree I can bath as long as I don't soak the stitch. I can live with that rule, so I don't bend it. I half-bath. That's what I call it when I'm not allowed to soak all of me.

With my broken leg, I propped the stitched parts on a black folding-step stool, also known as the pee stool in our house. For my newest ordeal, I don't need the pee stool. I just don't sink in up to my chin. Everything from ribs up stays above the water line because that's where the stitches are. Anything stitched must stay out, which, now that I'm over forty, is more often than when I was under thirty. I didn't break a bone or have a stitch before I was thirty-three. Then I had kids and my parts started falling apart, my body bravely trying to keep up with my ambition.

Salmon are similar. They frantically pitch into their life cycle, fully committed to the complicated process while trying to stay ahead of the fall-apart. Their eight-hundred-fifty-mile migration from the Pacific Ocean to Idaho is mindboggling. No wonder only a few dozen Chinook salmon make it to the finish line, mile eight hundred fifty, stashed deep in central Idaho wilderness. The odds are impossible, but they keep going. So do I.

Truthfully, this time I retreated to the tub because I was bored. My husband is teaching our boys how to shave the few hairs they have on their faces. I shave legs, not faces—my razor skills aren't needed. They kicked me out of their bathroom so I'm alone in mine. They're in the hallway bath that shares a wall with the bath in the master bedroom. I can hear their muffled banter through the barrier.

"Woah," my husband says. "You have a lot of shaving cream on your hands and none on your face."

I laugh imagining the white-foam mess expanding on the other side of the wall. My laugh surprises me because I haven't laughed in a few days. I'm stitched again and I'm not happy about it. I'm also grounded to the couch again just like I was when I had to learn to live with a rod in my right leg. Sitting still makes me anxious and keeping my heart rate low is unfulfilling, so to the tub to do nothing I go, where I do my best thinking.

On this particular night—the night I reduced my pain pills and hovered between oblivion and reality for the first time in a week—nothing turned into everything. Everything you're about to read. That really is something.

Now, about those fish. . . .

# PART I:

## Columbia River

# UNSCREWED

"YOU READY?"

"Yes."

"This is going to sting," Doc says while inserting a needle in my right ankle above the bone I occasionally (and unintentionally) knock with my other foot. Five people lean in. Four are staff, and one is my husband.

"You feel that?"

Doc's flicking my toes. I'm feeling nothing.

The needle sending numbness through my foot is nothing compared to what's coming next. A drill—a manually spun drill because a motor would strip the screw. The screw has to come out. Stripping it would stop that, then I'd have to go to the hospital, and I don't want to go to the hospital. Now that I'm numb, no one else wants me to go to the hospital either. I chose to do this so they're choosing to watch. They're about to see a patient come unglued as she's unscrewed. Something inside of me is coming out while I'm awake. Who would choose such an atrocity? Me. Wholeheartedly me. That's how badly I don't want drugs, how much I don't want to go under.

When a hockey puck hit my shin, breaking my leg in three places six months ago, I lived on drugs. Pills blocked pain, movement, infection, memory, and appetite. I remembered little and kept down even less. Narcotics stole food from my belly and thoughts from my head. I didn't move, didn't live, but I grew bone around a rod, so there's that.

Rod, the titanium invader in my right leg that rebuilt my lower limb, is staying inside me. So are two screws that hold him in place. There's actually three screws with him, one by my knee and two by my ankle, but one has to go. It's too big now that the swelling is gone. It's scraping my skin from the inside out by my ankle. When my son accidentally dinged it with a golf ball at a mini course a few weeks ago, I fell instantly into the fetal position on a publicly soiled, never washed, fake green lawn.

Even despite my nerves, I'm so ready. I'd rather do this awake than go under at the hospital or go fetal in public again. Besides, this injury is old news. I'm over it, so let's get on with it. I'm too focused on planning a road trip of epic potential. There will be no limping from the ocean to Idaho.

"I'm going to cut your skin along the original insertion scar, unscrew the screw, then sew you up," Doc says. "The unscrewing takes two minutes tops. Ready?"

"Ready," I say, lying back on the crinkly, paper-covered hospital table.

I'm squeezing my husband's hand and staring at white-speckled, square ceiling tiles while my shoulder blades feel the metal table through the noisy, flimsy tissue paper every patient must lie on for any procedure. Doc and staff are down by my ankle, drilling. I can't see what Doc's doing, but I can feel it. It's tremendous pressure, the pushing of the manual screwdriver spinning counterclockwise against my tibia. The intensity grows as I question why I chose two minutes of torture over two days of whacked on drugs, but I grit my teeth and squeeze harder.

I tell myself I've got this when I hear Doc set down the drill, but no. He's not done. He's adjusting his hold. There's a dab of scar tissue in the way, so he's choking up on the grip. I'm only half-unscrewed.

My back, no longer flat on the table, arches as if I have defibrillating shock paddles charged to my chest as he continues. My body strains toward the ceiling, no reprieve until the screw is unscrewed. I don't pass out, but I lose my manners, muttering vulgar words. A lot of bad words. Someone holds down my strong, kicking left leg, and I nearly break my husband's hand with one hand while shredding the tissue paper under my butt with my other hand.

"Stay with me," Doc says. "Almost there."

I'm certain the ticker passes two minutes before the pressure eases. Stainless steel tools rattle on the tray. Drill done. Sutures.

"You still with me?" he asks while concentrating on sewing me up.

My stiffened back relaxes into the table. I want to yell, "Screw you!" But I'm out of adrenaline.

"Kris, you okay?" Doc asks again. "I need an answer."

"Her hand is still squeezing mine," my husband says. "She's in there."

I call my husband Hotness when I'm not getting unscrewed. That name was inspired by my drug daze some months back when I was growing bone on the couch. I made the change in my phone when I wasn't supposed to have my phone. With no memory retention, I had no idea who "Hotness" was when he started texting me a few days later to check on me while he was at work. The nickname stuck. He's still Hotness in my phone and around the house.

I could feel my ever-tightening fist crushing his finger bones mere seconds ago. I've never had such a grip or that deep an arch in my back. I'm sick of ceilings, staring up at them. The tile kind and the glass kind. The tile kind means you're sick. The glass kind means career-crusher imminent. Shatter it. Sit up.

"I'm with you," I say sitting up.

Everyone leans back, assessing my delirium as I pull myself up to a seated position, leaving my lower half prone. I'm not walk-ready yet. I need to find my head first. I see the stitches before asking for the screw. That's how fast I find my head. My new leg is worth one hundred thousand dollars, screw included. That screw is going home with me, my reminder on bad days that there's always something worse.

# *PAIN*DEMIC

SOMETHING WORSE COMES less than a year later—for everyone, not just for me. A global pandemic. I started researching my next major outdoor story, a film project, shortly after I was unscrewed and shortly before COVID-19 undid all of us.

Research involves a lot of phone time in sit-position, so I have to stretch my rebuilt leg often. I walk without a limp, and I can even run some, so to break up research blocks of sitting for hours at a time, I craft my own recovery race. I call it my Tri-20 in 2020. Swim twenty laps, bike twenty dirt miles, and run twenty trail miles. I bike before running because I need to bulk up my right leg before I pound dirt with it. And I swim before biking because it's the least amount of impact on my weak limb. It's so weak that I spend the first month in the pool swimming in circles. My right side is no help, and my left side is overambitious. Swimming lap lanes in circle formation is laughable, but by the time I'm strong enough to do ten laps, I level to a weave between the ropes rather than full circles. That's how I know I'm getting stronger. Plus, the lifeguard finally sits down. He paced the end of my lane in retrieve-mode for six weeks while I learned, looking like I was drowning.

I swim twenty laps the day before the city pool closes indefinitely because of COVID-19. I'm not a pretty swimmer or a fast swimmer, but for the first time in my life I'm a head-underwater swimmer. I learned how to ration my breaths, kick in nearly a straight line, and securely suction cup goggles to my face so I could swim with my contacts in. Sure, I could surface myself as needed before, but I used to hate swimming with my head underwater. I don't anymore. I'm going to be studying something that lives 100 percent of its life underwater; I should at least know how to put my head underwater without having a panic attack.

The bike is more comfortable than the pool right from the start, but I struggle with so much time in the saddle and with being alone on my bike. I seem to attract a lot of thorns, which means I get a lot of flat tires when I'm out of aid range. The bike shop is closed so they can't fix my flats, and I don't know how to fix them myself. But I need my flat tires fixed so I can pedal away from the worries of our world, in search of some speck of normal. We all need that when it feels like the world is reeling. If I'm going to do this bike thing, I'm going to change tires.

When customers stopped going into stores, employees started coming to our doors. Social media helps us all connect while we become increasingly isolated, so when my local bike shop posts about their new mobile service, I order a tire tube. The shop manager says his store is empty, but his new mobile business is record breaking. Adapt to persist. This is humanity working with what it's got and making it.

He had a tube on my porch later that same day. It was delivered to the wrong porch the first time—store clerks largely unaccustomed to mobile transactions and all—but eventually it showed up on my porch. I spend several nights in my driveway, wallowing in dirt and grease, teaching myself how to repair my bike and to change its tires. It becomes my proof of self-sufficiency in the chaos of global helplessness.

I ache for assignments that could send me into the field for stories that pay, but they don't develop like the bike shop's delivery service does, so I write about porch stargazers and backyard birders. I start keeping my camera on the kitchen table too. I shoot photos of birds while eating breakfast. I use the white wood shutters over the window as my cover. It works well. I watch magpies, sparrows, finches, and robins collect nest material from my flowerbeds.

I also saw my first Steller's jay a few days ago. I don't have a birding life list, but seeing new wildlife where I live with the outdoor work that I do is rare, so it was a momentous morning. So was the morning I sat on my front porch with my video camera, trying to figure out what was ringing through the neighborhood. It was so quiet on our street—no new house construction, no traffic, no mowers—that the ringing was a welcome ruckus while the world waited for the pandemic to pass. At first, I thought my neighbor's air conditioner was broken, but it was too cold for that to be on. A loose chain on my drift boat's trailer? I wondered. Nothing was loose, but those finches I photographed during breakfast were stealing threads from my boat cover. I put duct tape over the frayed parts. They beaked through it before lunch.

I listened to the ringing for two hours, then I finally saw the source. And what a sight to behold: life going on despite ours being on hold. A starling was making its nest in my neighbor's basketball stand made of hollowed out steel. The ringing was the bird's talons scratching the inside of the stand, while situating its new home for soon-to-arrive eggs. The ringing stopped when the bird popped its head out the top in anticipation of liftoff for more filler. I shot video of the back and forth with ring between.

Now I have a starling movie, and my first Steller's jay sighting under my belt. Plus I can change bike tires, and I have toilet paper. Not everyone can say that. What a crazy fetish. The manager of the grocery store I'm faithful to called the morning he had a wad. He hid it in his back office for us, the exchange reminiscent of illicit, smuggled goods. We don't hoard, but we bought a pack from him. It's so see-through-thin and one-ply that we dread using it when our pre-pandemic rolls run out.

I'm so dreading it that when my youngest son starts blowing his nose in tissue bunches that are so big they pass as paper roses, I tell it to him straight. He doesn't have COVID-19. He has allergies, and isolation started in March when his nose runs rich with spring pollen. On garbage day, I find his can full of tissue, so we must have a dinner-table talk. That's where we discuss all the things we don't have time to hash out during the day.

"Son, I know it's fun to be out of school when you should be in. I know it's fun to screen time in your pajamas. I know it's fun to eat whenever, sleep whenever, and game whenever, but you know what's not fun? Running out of toilet paper. These are pandemic times, kid, and toilet paper is precious for some weird, unexplainable reason. Everyone wants it. Lots of it. Lots more of it than they need, and they're going to hoard it until the 'P' word goes away." By "P," I was referring to the pandemic—no bathroom euphemisms.

"That doesn't make any sense," he says, scowling at me as if the words coming out of my mouth are ridiculous. He's not wrong. A run on TP? Yeah, ridiculous.

"Nothing makes sense right now, baby boy," I continue. (His older brother is "big boy.") "This is not our planet's first pandemic, but it is our first pandemic—and most everyone else's first pandemic too. No one knows how to properly behave, panic is close to the surface, crazy is on full display, and toilet paper seems to be the soothe-all."

"Why are you telling me this?" he asks, wanting me to get to the point so he can eat his corn mush before it gets cold. Creamed corn is corn mush according to him.

"Because you're using too much toilet paper for pandemic times. I know everything feels uncertain, but one thing is for certain. You are going to have to choose between wiping your nose and wiping your butt."

I'm giving him an ultimatum. I can see the disbelief on his astonished face, so I continue while I have him engaged.

"I'm down to three squares for pee. All of us are down to five squares for poop. You're taking away from our bathroom needs by shoving rose-sized wads of tissue up your nose for snot. We are not giving up our squares for your nose. Time for a handkerchief. Make sure it's in the wash every week."

We ration our squares, but we embellish dessert. We go from eating that extra special course at the end of a meal once a week to once a day. And if it's one of our birthdays, dessert is the meal. Bubble gum ice cream with chocolate cake for me on my April birthday.

It takes a while for the sweets to catch up to my seat, but they do, so I increase bike miles to compensate for comfort food. I ride so far that my butt bones are chapped and sore. I ride for so many weeks, my desert route reveals rattlesnakes as the frost recedes. When I conquer twenty miles by bike, I switch to running. I use the same trail for my twenty-mile run, but decide my twenty-miler is my last desert run until the snow returns. Way too many rattlers for a calm session. I'm getting out and staying upright, but I want to be farther out now that both legs work, and I've completed my Tri-20, marking my recovery officially complete.

I also want to go farther out because, unless I'm riding or running, I'm inside. And my family is inside. We are together non-stop during quarantine. The stack of board games we brought up from the basement turn from quaint to boring. The puzzles, pointless. Building a horseshoe pit in the back-yard eats a few days, and so does building new garden beds and street hockey in the driveway. None of us do our hair, my mascara dries up in its tube from lack of application to my eyelashes, and we wear the same clothes for days in a row. At least I'm saving money on make-up, and there's only one load of laundry on wash day.

When school officially ends for my boys as students and my husband as a teacher, I really feel together-time overload. I'm trying to find work when it feels as if the world can't work. I'm scrambling for normal, and I won't get it when everyone else has been sucked out of their routines. It feels rude to admit it, but I want alone time. Not family time. Alone time. Time to figure out how to get through something that's making millions sick and killing millions more.

I want to wear my worries where no one can see me because we wear brave faces in the space we call home. We listen to music when we clean house every Sunday. The tunes are in shuffle mode, but every time a live-recorded song plays, I want to push skip. Hearing so many people cheering, singing, touching in close quarters, celebrating together makes my eyes burn. Emotion randomly leaks out while I vacuum. We don't miss the crowd at a concert or the beer in a bar until we're not allowed to experience either. I want to roam—not run away, just roam. Roam alone where worry lines replace laugh lines and no one is around to ask me why.

Roaming is a big ask with the whole country shut down. Tracking the 850-mile migration of a disappearing fish is a bigger ask, but I'm intrigued. Decision made. I'll be following salmon from the ocean to Idaho. Easier said than done, but I know that once I say it, I'll do it. I want to and I have to.

I lost 60 percent of my business as a self-employed free-lance journalist while growing bone on the couch. I wasn't in the field shooting stories. I need to recover lost time and lost money for my family's sake and for mine. I choose Chinook salmon, the kings of the Pacific Northwest, as my saving grace. They migrate through four rivers and three states twice to lay eggs once. I want to see the whole process, not just the finish line in Idaho, and I want to show it to everyone else.

I apply for thirteen journalism grants. I win zero. I keep applying. I secure one funder, Toyota. I keep planning. Then the pandemic does more than hit. It explodes. Just when I'm about to go out, we all have to come in. At least this time I'm not the only person grounded to the couch. We all are as COVID-19 invades more than our bodies.

Some media outlets that were already financially fragile close for good. Others stop payment on pending stories and freeze funds for future stories. If you're not covering the pandemic, they don't want to hear from you, and if they don't have the budget to cover the pandemic, they're not hearing from anyone; they're closed, most likely bankrupt due to lack of advertisers, never to reopen.

The pandemic turns my recovery project into my only project as quickly as a finger-snap, leaving me with a downtrend for two years instead of one. It's a disappointing realization. My boys are sent home for school on a screen. My wireless mouse unintentionally connects to the computer in their room above my office—a funny realization that clusters productivity for all of us quickly. My husband is working from home too, struggling to connect with special needs kids without holding their hands. A frustrating realization. We go to the store every two weeks. We watch movies every day. Everyone feels the pains of the pandemic—physically, emotionally, financially, socially. We've spiraled into an all-consuming *pain*demic.

My desire to follow fish grows as orders to stay home continue. We aren't moving, but the fish are. I need a house on wheels. It took me three months to partner with Toyota. It takes me two weeks to find Four Wheel Campers and secure somewhere safe for me to travel responsibly while also isolating as I cross state lines during a pandemic. The fish are moving, and now so am I. I'm pulling off the impossible during an impossible time for our planet.

The truck, wrapped in the fin print of Chinook salmon, arrives one day in early June. It pairs with the camper the next day, and I drive to the Oregon coast the day after. I have one thermometer, two large jugs of disinfecting wipes, three double-sided masks hand-sewn by my step-mo[...] four layers of clothes, and five cameras.

I've established pre-arranged, secure overnight spo[...] They're offered by hosts I haven't met who live along the route. They're my safe havens as I work my way across the Pacific Northwest in uncertain times. I call these spots D&Ds. Instead of B&Bs for "bed and breakfasts," D&D is my acronym for "drive in at sunset and dash out at sunrise." I do this nightly on closed boat ramps, empty fields, and private driveways. I don't see my hosts, but they know I'm on schedule via text. While I'm on the road alone, this eases my husband and me, too, if I'm honest with you, which I am. I'll sit with uncomfortable, but I won't sit with unsafe. I've crafted the safest plan for working during a pandemic. I'm self-contained in my rig. I'm ready.

You ready? Stay with me.

ber-in-law,

s.

# SALT

SALMON HATCH IN their home water, grow to finger-length, then rush with spring runoff to the ocean, which is where I'm heading. They survive in saltwater for a few years even though their first gulps are freshwater. Imagine that detox process. Food is more plentiful in the ocean, so they grow bigger. That's why they're out there, to grow. When they're longer than your arm, they switch their operating system from saltwater back to fresh—another mind-boggling detox. In returning home, they swim to high mountain streams with zero salt to their cribs, where they leave eggs before departing this world. They die. There's no reset. No do-over. Death is certain. They fall apart on the way back home yet they're all in, doing everything as if it's their last chance. Because it is.

I feel like this is my last chance, too—my last chance to see them anyway. Salmon don't make it home en masse anymore. That's what they used to do, what they were made to do. To move en masse and feed the masses. Native American tribes throughout the Pacific Northwest relied on salmon feasts for subsistence, but they don't anymore. There's not enough fish. The list of reasons is longer than the list Santa checks twice.

I've never touched a salmon in Idaho and I don't need to. One doesn't even need to nip my fly line when I'm fishing. I just want to know they're here, and they are. Barely. That's why I'm running out of chances. I want to see their migration before they're gone. I want to show you their migration before it's gone. And gone is where it's going if we don't shorten that list.

I'm about to see all 850 miles of the migration route. Every help and every hurdle. Everything fish face. I'm so eager, I only stop for gas once on my way to Oregon. Trucks ride a bit differently with a house in their bed, so I'll have to be more fuel conscious than usual.

Other than conducting interviews, fueling is my only contact with society. When you travel isolated during a pandemic, you must also travel prepared. Everything I need to do my job is in the backseat of my truck. Everything I need to stay alive is in the bed of that same truck. After the gas station stop five hours into my drive, I sanitize my hands and don't stop again until I reach the coast.

Cassi Wood is the first person I think of when I stick my rubber-booted feet in the cold flow of the Pacific Ocean. She's already at the end of the route, where I'll see her in August. She's one of the reasons I'm standing at the start in June with the Blue Ridge mountains throwing chilled colors at my back. No warm hues on this coast. Even the black wall of rock breaking waves around the beach has a dense, cold vibe.

Cassi is an Idaho-born fisheries biologist. She has the confidence of a net-full angler carrying a head full of science on her shoulders. She knows how deep fishing holes should be, how far bends should curve, and how many logs to submerge to entice fish. She showed me the end of this migration route a few years ago, and here I stand at the beginning of it. Fish on their way home this year are descendants of the Chinook we saw together while lying on a beaver dam at mile 850. They're migrating to Idaho just like I'm about to.

My launch pad is the mouth of the Columbia River where it opens to the ocean. Anyone can come here. It's inside Fort Stevens State Park, but no one is coming here while I'm here because of the pandemic. I'm alone on the beach, so I'm not wearing a mask. I'm full face to the unfriendly weather. Is it possible the Oregon coast is colder in June than Idaho is in January? Totally possible. I have on every layer I brought, plus gloves.

The coast is deserted like that beaver dam was. The memory resurfaces as I watch saltwater foam at my feet while visualizing freshwater below my chin. That's how close I was to the water as I quietly crawled along the beaver dam with an underwater camera strapped to a melon-sized stone.

I reached the middle of the logjam and dropped my rock cam in the river behind it. I lay low on my belly unseen, waiting for the wild to approach. Cassi hid alongside me. We were both in waders, hair tucked in ballcaps.

We'd spent three days documenting the Yankee Fork of the Salmon River in central Idaho. Chinook rushed there by the thousands before miners rushed in. The Yankee Fork was ripped open for gold seven decades ago—a century after the California Gold Rush. California may have produced the most gold starting in the 1850s, but its rush was over when Idaho's started in 1860, and to this day, miners still seek its riches. Idaho is the Gem State, not the potato state, because miners opened its heart—not farmers. They came for gold at first, then silver, then phosphate, and on it goes today.

For twenty years, my family and I have hauled into the same woods with a permit in one hand and a saw in the other to cut our own Christmas tree. In 2020, our family tradition died. Not because of the pandemic, but because of a pit. There's a new mine in our grove. We'll spend the summer looking for somewhere else to go so we can revive the tradition elsewhere when snow returns.

Miners aren't done with Idaho because its source isn't depleted. It's ever out of reach yet ever sought. Remote country doesn't give willingly, but the Yankee Fork was accessible and rich with gold, so dredge they did in the 1940s.

Salmon lost their beds during the dredge era, but they're slowly trickling back between the overturned stones. That's what the gravel piles are, the river's guts ripped out for gold. The Yankee Fork Gold Dredge turned the drainage inside out in search of precious metal. The rock it spit in the process is piled for seven miles. Old mining towns and lumber mills mark the land too. The age of resource extraction and Western expansion on raw display, humanity's black eye.

The historic upheaval has long since passed, but the Yankee Fork hasn't recovered. The dredge is still sitting in there. It looks as if the stalled machine will start churning earth again, but it won't. A shift in society's priorities has the wild winning the watershed once again. We're gradually rolling out a restored welcome mat for fish and wildlife. It's story worthy. That's why I was lying on a beaver dam watching a rotting fish hold reign—documenting proof of pivot in a cold-water fishery that was once, and will be again, a hotbed for Chinook salmon programmed to make it home no matter how many miles, or metals, are in their way.

The fish in the watering hole behind the beaver dam sported a bruised snout and threadbare fins. It was upstream of the dam, and my camera had a clear shot. I let it roll as the fish circled unaware of being watched. The badges of the brutal 850-mile journey were evident. It was beat, not just at the ends but totally beat from tip to tail. The decaying yet defensive fish hovered over its young, protecting new life while on its death bed.

Salmon die when they're done spawning. Spawning is the scientific term for mating. Yes, salmon sex—the last thing a salmon does after swimming all the way to the ocean, growing big and swimming all the way back to where it was born is spawn. A one-time affair. Salmon make babies, then die. That's it. They ensure future fish, stop fighting the current, then float away, putting all their eggs in the river's basket. They feed the forest as they decompose too.

That part of the story is several hundred miles away, and I have yet to understand it. But as I revisit the condition of that first fish in my mind, the one by the beaver dam at the final mile, I'm reminded of my original curiosity. What happened to that fish? It was in terrible shape. But really, who wouldn't look like a zombie after swimming that far?

I've since learned that there's more to it than distance and I guarantee the route looks nothing like it did a century ago. Changes. So many changes. What does a fish go through to get home? What are the helps and hurdles? How is migration even possible with all of us demanding so many other things from our natural resources? I know what the end of the journey looks like. Let's find the beginning. Let's solve the puzzle. Tell the story.

As I swap river for ocean in my mind, I begin to taste salt on my lips. I declare to the seagulls above and the seaweed below, "I am following salmon migration from the ocean to Idaho. This is mile 0."

# GORGED

MILE 0 TO Bonneville Lock and Dam, at mile 146, is considered an estuary because it's a mix of saltwater and freshwater influenced by ocean tide. On that long Santa list of issues I mentioned, ocean ranks high on the risk scale. Young salmon that flush to the ocean to grow up face a hostile environment in saltwater. Everything wants to eat salmon, including us. Whales, seals, and seagulls have always eaten salmon, but the food chain has a kink. Salmon are dying off, and there are now more dangers in the ocean than predators. Our garbage washes out to sea, a sea that's getting warmer. Warmer water changes meals. It's the difference between what's on the menu in North Dakota versus New Mexico. Warmer places equal warmer food. The same applies in the ocean, and salmon, looking for cold-water food to consume, face diet changes as water warms and more of our pollution washes out.

Hurdles become harder to clear when the environment evolves faster than we do. Migration patterns shift as seasons change with rising temperature. It's not about where the wild things are anymore—it's about where the wild things are going. We have less snow and more summer, which means wildflowers bloom weeks earlier than they did in the 1970s and transit birds are showing up in regions that were once too harsh for them but are now considered mild.

Humans are shifting too. We're seeing that with the pandemic. People want to live where they feel safe. Between a global virus, wildfires, and hurricanes, both coasts no longer feel safe. The human population is pushing inland in search of safety, space, and unspoiled land. That's why addressing the loss of salmon is even harder in this century: we've exacerbated the unstable. Yes, the planet is ever-changing, but now it's changing in spite of us and because of us, and its changing faster than we can keep up. The same is true for wildlife.

Even if salmon had an unimpeded trip to the ocean, if that ocean is too hot or too dirty when they get there, a lot of them wouldn't make it back, anyway. What doesn't adapt doesn't last, no matter how many Band-Aids are applied.

Restored estuaries are more than Band-Aids; they're commitments to recovery. That's why they're important. The estuary I visit with Regan McNatt was a cow pasture ten years ago. Now it's a fish nursery like it was before we put hoof on it. Regan is a NOAA supervisory research fisheries biologist. She sees young fish on their way to the ocean buffeting in the backwater. She sees adult Chinook on their way back to Idaho resting in the estuary too.

"If you'd been here ten years ago, you would have seen cows grazing," she says. She's clad in waders and a ballcap while crouching low in marsh reeds to inspect insects, fish food. "Now you have channels, and you have fish that are in here eating and getting bigger, getting stronger so they can finish their migration."

Through the estuary stretch of the salmon migration route, fish find sanctuary, but it's short lived and only reasonably safe. Invaders are plentiful in brackish backwater for raising young fish and resting adult fish. White gulls circling over my head are a flock of twenty, each one snatching a finger-length fish in its beak.

Seventeen miles inland from the ocean, cormorants—a darker, larger bird—are nesting on the Astoria-Megler Bridge that spans the Lower Columbia River between Oregon and Washington. As I drive it, I wonder how other drivers contend with the birds diving too close to their windshields, hoods, tires. There are 5,100 nests on the bridge. They're not supposed to be there. They weren't supposed to be on the island they were hazed from either, but here they are, surviving on salmon while swooping through traffic.

With at least two birds per nest eating fifteen fish a day, that's 153,000 fish dying daily. That's why Chris Rodriguez shows me the bridge of birds. His if-it's-not-one-thing-it's-another perspective claws for camera time. Chris is a technician with Oregon Department of Fish and Wildlife. While he's improving one thing, another is degrading—so he hears from frustrated people daily. Not enough fish, too many birds, not enough management, too much bureaucracy.

"The hardest part about my job is when salmon runs are low, frontline workers like us get the brunt of the complaints from the public," Chris says. "They want answers I can't provide and probably nobody can provide. It's frustrating when we expect a certain amount of fish to come back and they don't."

Chris keeps his hair shaved to stubble, nearly bald. I wonder if he does that so he's not tempted to pull it out because I imagine there are days when he would if it were longer. Frontline workers, the people who work with the public, are first in line for rants. It's hard to comprehend the awkwardness of such a position unless you witness one of these rants firsthand. I witnessed one once in Yellowstone National Park. I've witnessed many due to the nature of my work, but this one in particular is a vivid memory.

"This is your fault!" said the tourist in a fishing vest pointing a finger. "You screwed up! You should have done something earlier."

This is how Todd Koel's day started. It's how my day started, too, but I wasn't on the receiving end of the pointed finger, rather the recording end of the incident.

Todd, prepping his boat on the ramp into Yellowstone Lake, didn't fold his arms over his chest defensively. He didn't walk away, and he didn't interrupt. There was no reason to. After tossing such harsh accusations, the tourist wouldn't care what Todd had to say. He was just making sure he had Todd's ear and the media's eye. My stomach felt a bit sour because Todd's day may have started better if my lens wasn't on him. That made him an obvious target for someone ready to rant. The know-I'm-angry angler was trying to embarrass the knows-what-he's-doing biologist in front of the nosey reporters. His intentions were so blatantly devious that I felt embarrassed for him.

Todd is Yellowstone National Park's native fish conservation leader. On a clear-sky, summer morning, a mad park visitor laid into him about the park's lake trout problem. Todd, with thick chestnut-colored hair tamed by a walnut-shade inspired

NPS-issued ballcap, kept his cool while the visitor spouted at him. When the yeller finished, Todd calmly acknowledged the problem, telling the guy what the nets on his boat do (remove lake trout by the hundreds in one swoop) before climbing on board. Regardless of the unscheduled protest, we left port on time.

As Todd slowly motored his jetboat out of the no-wake zone, he looked back at the tourist on the ramp then casted a glance at me and the rest of the media in his boat. He looked next at the water, fishing for words, then back to us again, before stunning us with one sentence. One thread of understanding, shared emotion between opposing sides.

"There is a lot of passion involved when it comes to the park," Todd said.

Same kind of confrontations happen because of salmon, only it's Chris on the ramp in Oregon instead of Todd on the ramp in Yellowstone. The lake trout invasion in the nation's first national park is not Todd's fault. He didn't screw up, but he is doing something about it now. That's why there's a commercial fishing crew from the Great Lakes region catching lake trout with up to forty miles of netting. It operates in the epicenter of the visitor's anger. Lake trout are not native to the park. An angler caught the first one in 1994. By the mid-2000s, lake trout had eaten up to 95 percent of the native Yellowstone cutthroat trout in Yellowstone Lake.

"The problem is lake trout are like large wolves on the landscape, only in the lake," Todd said. "Large, highly predatory, fish-eating machines, essentially."

Commercial gillnetting to kill lake trout went gangbusters starting in 2009. From May through October, three hundred thousand lake trout are netted, killed, and dumped back into the lake as decomposing nutrients. The effort is time intensive and wallet consuming, costing two million dollars annually.

The goal is to crash the lake trout population so cutthroat trout can come back. The crash is close. After a decade of concentrated effort, the fishery has begun to show signs of change. An estimated forty other types of wildlife consider cutthroat trout part of their diet. When those fish disappeared, the animals left the lake. Now, eagles are circling and grizzlies are back on the banks.

Their return coincides with the black bins on the gillnetting boat. Hundreds of dead lake trout are in the bins, brought in while more netting goes out. Todd cut a lake trout belly open to find eight small cutthroats inside. With so many fish still coming on board, it's hard to see a population crash coming, but Todd was convinced it would. The tide had already begun to turn, despite tourists yelling at him on the boat ramp.

"What I really love about it is just knowing we are making positive change at a time when if we weren't doing some of these things maybe ten, twenty, thirty years from now, [cutthroats] would be gone," Todd said. "We're just doing things right at the right time. We are making a big difference that will last long-term for a lot of other people into the future."

If you catch a cutthroat trout, you must put it back. If you catch a lake trout, you can keep it. In fact, you have to. There's a mandatory kill order on lake trout, and there's no limit. Between angler harvest and intense netting, lunkers are taking a punch in the gills.

Lake trout aren't eating salmon in the Columbia River, but everything else is—birds closer to the ocean and seals closer to the dams. These animals want an easy meal, and they have the advantage when there's a wall in the water. That's what dams are: walls. And in the Gorge, Bonneville Dam is the only wall that isn't green. Decades of moisture build-up make the dam look black-rock-slick with dark moss, but the rest of the Columbia River Gorge, near Portland, is misty-green gorgeous. I arrive in the Gorge on the heels of an afternoon storm. It's grand magnificence. Every shade of green from river to ridge screams, "point your lens here," and I want it all on record right away. The finely sifted clouds clinging to Beacon Rock, the prominent landmark seen by Lewis and Clark in 1805 and by Indigenous people for centuries before that, has significant placement in the Gorge. The thick emerald carpet of moss down low by the river keeps with the green theme as does the veil of shamrock, shaded foliage up higher.

My basecamp in the Gorge is a closed boat ramp. There's a sign at the top of the ramp. It's hand painted with yellow letters brushed over blue background reading, "Practice Social Distancing." I am indeed doing that, since I'm the only one allowed to camp here overnight, and I interact with my host by text, so she knows when I come and go during the dark hours.

During the day, I work the corridor between the ocean and Bonneville Dam. I meet commercial fishers and sport fishers, both of whom feel the impact of shrinking salmon runs. Canneries that used to keep the coast in business by packaging millions of salmon as food for the masses closed decades ago. Steven Fick's fish packing plant sits on the footprint of one of the last canneries on the coast, its rotted, raised beams sticking out of the shallows next to his shop. He expects to process a couple hundred Chinook salmon daily. On the day I'm with him, there are only ten.

"We want to improve harvest opportunities through whatever tools we have available to us so that we can get fish to the public," Steve says, watching his crew process the ten fish for market. "We recognize that for some of this the damage has been done, and you're not going to bring it back, but what you want strategically is a lot of people fighting for the same cause. You don't want to get rid of advocates for natural resources."

One of those advocates is Kyle Jones. He's a lifelong salmon fisherman and fishing guide from Idaho who works the entire Columbia River Basin to find year-round work because his favorite holes flipped from salmon to walleye five years ago. The tide is turning on his sport-fishing business.

"I have a love-hate relationship with walleye," Kyle says. "They've saved my business. They've fed my family, but if I could have my pick, no. It would be salmon. Salmon are meant to be here."

Both Steve and Kyle harvest fish. In the Gorge, a lot of people harvest fish, including salmon. Reducing harvest isn't increasing returns. It's a crummy situation in a captivating place where "beautiful" is an understatement, and wet is the norm. There's nothing dry about the Gorge.

I quickly realize I didn't arrive on the heels of rain. This place always looks puddled, and I'm gorged on it by day two. I need sun or my sunny disposition suffers. I'm sad and sleepy here. Lack of light and lack of rest are wearing on me too early in the trip.

Drips drop on my camper roof overnight, keeping me awake. In the dark, it's hard to tell if it's currently raining, or if rain from the last storm is slipping from the saturated canopy above my rig. There's so much moisture collecting in the Gorge, the air smells wet. My notebook is constantly damp, and I fight fog from my lens constantly. If it isn't raining, it's about to rain, so I live in my rubber coat and rubber boots for four days. I only de-layer when I enter my camper at night. The solar panels on the roof of my rig collect enough watts to cook my dinner and charge my batteries, but there's a marked difference in energy storage levels. In sunshine, no-shade places, I collect double the watts than when I'm working in the cloudy, shady Gorge, where the solar source is sporadic. River always flows, but the sun doesn't always shine. That's why hydropower has favor here, especially when it's generated at dams like the one in the Gorge.

While the sight of the Gorge astounds me—it's like a rainforest in an otherwise desert West—it's the sounds that overwhelm me. The scenery slowly swishes quietly in the space between sky and ground with soft, take-your-time visuals, but all of that splendor is set to a soundtrack that's out of sync.

What I see deserves wispy ethereal notes. Instead, it's truck and train traffic rumbling up the ribs of the river on both sides and barges cutting through the middle. The highway hum is never-ending, even at three a.m., and if it's not a train whistle waking you up on the north side of the river, it's the horn of a long-haul diesel on the south side of it. How do people sleep here? They must be used to it, the white noise within the green their lullaby. It's as if the Gorge is so gorgeous, they put up with the acoustics for the aesthetics.

# WALLS

BONNEVILLE DAM IS closed to everyone but me and the five people following me around. They're the entourage of U.S. Army Corps of Engineers (USACE) granting me access and giving me a tour. The eight major dams in the Columbia River Basin that I need to see are closed. I will see all of them, but I concede repetition and push for entry into only one. The first one, Bonneville Dam, was completed in 1938.

A magnificent feat of engineering erected nearly a century ago, it's one of the state's most popular tourist attractions today but off-limits to the public during the pandemic. It continues to operate out of necessity, but social distancing dictates the crowd must stay away. The freeway exits through this area are closed. For the public, there's no reason to get off if nothing is open, but I have clearance to exit so I pull in.

The dam is vacant just like the beach was. It feels strange working in an empty world—like doomsday is approaching. I'm lucky to see five strangers in person in one place. We're almost party giddy to be socializing six feet apart, even though we don't know what the lower half of each other's faces look like. Gatherings haven't happened in months, and I had to show my temperature, sanitize my gear, and keep my face covered to attend this one.

Amy Echols made the meeting possible. She's USACE's Northwestern Division outreach coordinator. After being transferred to nearly every public relations person the Corps has on staff—and there are a lot—I landed in Amy's inbox. I knew she would make our meet happen. She's smart, stern, and in need of a haircut. She hasn't seen her hairdresser during the pandemic, and she quips about how she's long overdue for a cut and color. I don't mind, but she does. She keeps her sunglasses on her head like a headband holding her dark brown bangs back. The placement shows off her eyes, and eyes help audiences connect, so I let the sunglasses ride high during her interview.

Amy knows what I need to see, and I know not to ask for more than that. I want footage from within the dam, and she'll get me in as far as she can within Corps restrictions. When Amy called with approval for entry, I accepted the single June date she issued, eager to work with whatever she could show me. Access to a federally managed facility comes with restrictions. Double those restrictions during a pandemic. Sometimes you have to go with what you need instead of what you want. I want a lot more than I'm going to get, but I'll get what I need rather than bow out with nothing. And I know I'm not alone—it seems a lot of decisions during a global crisis cause us to accept what we need instead of getting what we want. Our new normal when the virus passes may cause us to trend that way permanently.

My number one ask in relation to the dam is to see where the counters work, the people who tally fish passing through the dams. I want to watch them work and ask them about what they see. My number one ask is denied. The room where the counters work isn't big enough for me to enter while maintaining the mandated social distance barrier. I interview the man who manages the counters instead, Bob Wertheimer. He's the U.S. Army Corps of Engineers' supervisory fish biologist out of the Portland District. He's totally into fish, making sure salmon pass the dam and the tallies are accurate.

"These species will persist," Bob says. "We've got a mandate not to jeopardize their existence. We take it very seriously."

My next ask is to see the window where fish pass—a dimly lit, cavernous space that's usually open to the public. Despite the unusual times, this ask is granted, and our group ventures to the room of windows as Amy, with her hair out of her eyes, explains the hydro hierarchy.

"The Corps owns and operates these dams, and Bonneville Power transmits and sells the hydropower generated from the dams," Amy says. "There are many people watching us and keeping us accountable and we say, 'Let them watch. That's a good thing.'"

Dams dictate flow. All dams have a reason for dictating flow, often several reasons, to justify the building costs. In Bonneville's case, the original purposes were, and still stand today as, hydropower and navigation. Flood control, irrigation, and recreation are factors, too, but they don't motivate a build like the other two reasons do.

Water passes through the wall, but not before those various purposes are satisfied. For power, the dam ramps up underwater force as energy to light your home. For navigation, the dam backs up flow to flush boat traffic up and down. For flood prevention, the dam holds back flow to make sure downstream cities like Portland don't drown like they used to.

To meet its purpose for existing, folds of fluted cement span the Columbia River at the site of Bonneville Dam. Chutes divide the flutes. Stand downstream of the dam and picture a stage. Looking at the stage from the far-left front row seat exposes the wings on the right side of the stage. What pours out of these wings is water instead of ballerinas.

What's in the water can't survive traveling through the wall with the water. That's why there are ladders around the wall. Salmon traveling to and from the Pacific Ocean struggle with these man-made wonders during their natural-born migration. Ladders help them pass the walls in the water. They're not ladders to the top floor like you're thinking. They're more like stairs with landings every few feet for resting before the next step. It takes a lot of rest for fish to pass a dam, and returning salmon go against the current the whole way so there's a lot of resistance.

At dam sites, that resistance builds. You can hear it. The force of fluid is loud—raise-your-voice-to-be-heard-over-it loud—and misty. Not the weather-induced romantic mist floating around the Gorge at all times. It's mechanical mist from water pushing through flutes and chutes with so much force that heavy spray vaults into the air around the dam continuously.

The other dam ruckus is fireworks. Well, the sound of fireworks. Flare guns and non-lethal cracker shells detonate intermittently. They interrupt my interviews. They steal my thunder when I'm talking on camera. They help fish. It's the Corps' hazing technique. The bangs and screeches of pyrotechnics pester birds circling downstream of the dam. They're hunting for disoriented fish, easy eats. Bugging the birds is supposed to give fish time to get their bearings in the water column after pipes and ladders shoot them past the dam, so they don't get snatched up and eaten as easy prey.

Hazing probably works for some birds, but not the osprey I watch on a ledge near the ladder. Its talons are gouging a fish that's straddling the wall like a saddle on a horse. From my vantage point, I can't tell if it's salmon or something else. The bird's beak plucks at its flesh, a meal above the water while fireworks explode above its head.

While the dam exterior scrambles in noisy frenzy, the dam interior is surprisingly quiet, library quiet. When it's closed, make that a heavily insulated library. When you're in the tub late at night, while the rest of the house is sleeping, silence rings in your ears. When you sink your whole body into the tub, and water fills your ears, you hear a different pitch of silence. A muffled silence with echo. That's what the space inside the dam sounds like, especially by the windows. They are, after all, underwater, so the aquatic pitch makes sense.

There's a lot of important stuff going on inside a dam, but it's not loud like out on the wall. Turbines are spinning, fish are laddering, and water is moving. All three are monitored by skeleton staff, which I never meet because they work in spaces too small for one more body. I don't wander without my tour guides, and I only see one other person on the inside—a carpet cleaner. Every building closed during the pandemic will be sanitized and sparkling when we re-enter our daily routines. That's the business to be in during a virus: cleaning. While I'm scraping by as a journalist, cleaners make a steady paycheck—at least for facilities that are still open.

I spot one other guy on the other side of the glass. We aren't sharing the same air like I'm sharing air with the carpet cleaner. He's masked. I'm masked. Move along. The guy on the other side of the glass wears black suspenders as he monitors turbines. He's in a huge waterless room driving a motorized cart down aisles. One wall of the room is glass so visitors on the viewing platform can see how water makes watts. The cart the guy drives looks like it's the size of a matchbox car next to a row of eight orange power-producing turbines arranged single file. The turbines are two times bigger than the blue city water tank on the hill. They're beyond giant. I imagine how big the hole for that installation had to be when Bonneville was built. Way beyond Olympic-sized swimming standards for sure. The cart looks so small and the turbines so large that the guy looks like an Oompa Loompa heading to Willy Wonka's chocolate pool to give it a mega-stir with an oversized spoon.

Interviews take thirty to sixty minutes, so I conduct them outside the dam, with fresh air filtering the germs passing between me and the dam personnel answering my questions. Interviews are vital for perspective, and as you can imagine, the perspective of the dam builders comes from a place of much pride. They're proud of what they've raised in the river because dams make the builders the boss. Dams don't let Mother Nature do her bidding. Dams meet needs this nation wanted, demanded, a century ago. Dams turn water into power, river into highway, and desert into field. Dams do exactly what they were built for, even after all these years and they are the career dreams of many men. They taxed the brains of the brilliant in the planning process, and they took the lives of contractors in the building phase. That's why dam builders don't turn into dam breakers, not even for salmon.

While it's true that dams have a life expectancy, they are not temporary, and they are not easy to break. They're not like the hand-patted moat circling a sand castle on the beach that gets wiped out with one wave. It takes years to build dams. It will take years to break them. Sediment, cement, and who knows what else would have to move before the fish could move through a dam instead of around it.

No doubt, dams are a wall in the water, but ladders, pipes, trucks, and barges help the dam builders move fish around the walls. They're proud of all those inventions too, as they indicate proof of progress for fish recovery. But in reality, they truly indicate proof of a problem we aren't fixing because fewer and fewer fish are making their way onto the ladders, pipes, trucks, and barges.

I watch the sincere efforts of staff shuffling fin and wonder if fish know this is not the way they want to go, even if it is the only way they can go. I recognize the many functions of the wall, its purpose for people, but it's still a wall in the way.

I study fish cycling through the system and think of spray paint. It's a weird pairing, but that's where I go in my head while the fish try to take on the wall. If they had a can of spray paint, what would they write, graffiti style, on the wall? The wall with windows so viewers can watch what must go around rather than through. And what about the windows in the walls? If the dam breaks, will I lose sight of what's right?

# WINDOWS

AT THE DAM, I spend more time inside at the windows than outside on the wall. The windows are the view into the fish ladder. Turbines and ladders came with the dam: the turbines to make power, the ladders to move fish around the wall that houses the turbines. The windows came a bit later but proved to be a brilliant move that allows humanity to see what's under the water, traveling to and from the ocean. It's like looking into an aquarium that hasn't been cleaned in six days. The water moves fast, but it's murky. It is river water, after all. There's a lot moving through it, including fish. When a fish enters a section of the underwater ladder that meets close to the glass of an underwater window, you'll see its silhouette. I'm searching for the moment when water, window, and salmon meet.

To get that shot, I burn through a lot of tape recording shoe-sized fish, or shad, as they dart up and down the ladder. Everything in the system must pass through, not just major migrators. I decide the more energy fish waste zooming in and out, the shorter their travel distance must be. They're releasing pent-up energy with all the back and forth, darting this way and that with no need for reserves. Maybe these are resident Gorge fish popping in for the day to see the foreigners—salmon—who are trying to pass through on their way to far flung, exotic places like Idaho.

I burn more tape on an eel-shaped lamprey suctioned to the glass with its front end while its back end waves in the current like a flag. I muse to myself about its travel log for the day: suck, slide one pane of glass that's about as wide as I am tall (5'4"), suck some more. While the smaller fish frenzy to go somewhere, anywhere, lamprey are in no hurry. They stick on the sidewall of the wet highway like they're napping. The tail waving action is mesmerizing, so I roll much longer than I need to, forgetting to push stop. I trance for a few minutes on the sidewinder while wondering how long it will take me to learn to talk through a mask without feeling muted or suffocated.

It's my first time around people I don't live with since the pandemic started. Other than the grocery store, it's my first trip out of the house since the pandemic started. It's also my first experience with conducting the business of open communication while hiding my face.

So much of what's said is lost behind fabric. Expressions, animations, wrinkles, dimples. On the plus side, some of what's lost should stay lost. That crusty booger peeking out of your left nostril. The chunk of fresh ground pepper trying to split your two front teeth like an excited five-year-old ballerina, clad in a yellow tutu and hair in a gel-spray slicked bun, poking her head through closed red curtains on the stage so she can see how many people showed up for her first dance recital. Grandma G. in the front row. . . . Focus, Kris. Stop masking and focus.

I stop rolling to find focus—my own, not the camera's. I'm having difficulty doing my job with my mask invading the lower third of everything I look at. Connecting with the subject will help. Touch the glass. I unhinge my camera from the tripod stationed five feet away from a window and walk toward the glass. I leave my tripod to hold my spot and hold my camera close to me, keeping it safe. It's a habit from years of shooting in crowds. There's no crowd here, no thieves either, but habits are tough to break.

There's a ledge at the bottom of the window. I set my camera sideways so its body is against my knees and won't fall off the ledge. With equipment secure, I lean my torso toward the glass, placing both hands on the smooth surface, feeling the cool thickness on the pads of my fingertips. The pane is solid, sturdy, and slightly vibrating. The technology of turning a river into a highway thrums through the clear divide.

The window I'm standing before looks in on steps of concrete covered with algae, like brown-green slime on the bottom of your kid's unkept fishbowl. The steps help salmon pass the dam in gradual succession: jump a step, rest, swim, jump the next step, repeat.

I want to ask the engineer who added the windows what his motivation was. Did he see salmon? Because I don't. Why does it take so long for one to appear in here when other fish are so frequent? It's a numbers game. The frequent fins have high numbers. With several species considered threatened, endangered, or extinct, salmon in the Pacific Northwest have dwindled significantly.

Several types of salmon are protected by the Endangered Species Act. As a nation, we've stopped the disappearance of other endangered species and righted humanity's wrong many times with this act. We've done it for bald eagles. We're doing it for grizzly bears. The next line here should be that we will do it for salmon. As I silently stare at the water on the other side of the window, I'm doubtful. I'm also mad. We're letting countless ecosystems down, from the ocean to Idaho, if salmon go extinct.

The situation is so dire, the Corps recently installed TV screens on the wall above the dam windows in Seattle. Older footage of swimming salmon plays on loop above window watchers, telling us over and over we're too late. What we want to see in the present is no longer here. Instead, it's on a screen, playing footage shot before the population tanked.

Seattle, Washington, is too far north for salmon swimming to Idaho. Idaho fish following the route I'm on start south of Seattle on the border of Oregon and Washington. There's no screen playing a loop of footage above the window I'm looking through. That tells me I'm not too late. What I want to see at present is here, and I will see it with my own eyes, not on a screen, if I stand here long enough. My timing is right; the salmon run is on. This is my best chance. I rest my forehead on the cool glass between my palms. Show up, fish. Show up.

With silent plea issued, I back away from the glass, walk back to my tripod, and click my camera in the locking plate on the top of my sticks. I'm back in work-mode, which involves a lot of staring. I have one long shot, ten minutes worth, of darters and wavers before the king arrives. I fidget during that time, thinking I'm so nervous, I'd be biting my nails if my teeth weren't hidden behind a mask. The guy on lookout two windows to my right is nervous too. It's Bob, the Corps fish biologist.

"The estimate for [2020] spring Chinook was forty thousand returning to Bonneville Dam. That's low," Bob says. "I want to see double or triple that. It scares me."

He's scared but hopeful. He knows improvements to the ladders in recent years mean more fish survive dam passage at Bonneville and beyond. The intersection of water, watts, and wildlife reoccur seven more times along the trek after fish pass the dam where Bob works.

I stop rolling to change my angle. Bob says Chinook usually swim deeper, lower in the window. I aim for the bottom third of the pane. Bob hollers across the viewing room that one's coming. The king is two windows away from me. The fish will be here in three . . . two . . . one . . . roll. I'm afraid it's too far from the window when I see nothing. I look high pane where the small fish dart, no biggie. I look low pane where the lamprey waves, before the king noses pane right, barely above the waver. The only thing closer to the glass is the suction part of the lamprey. The salmon is so close to the opaque barrier between us that murky is irrelevant. I see it. The king swims directly into view of my lens, jaws slightly open, fins sea worthy. Once you see the size and swagger of an adult Chinook, you'll never mistake small fish for salmon again.

All the fish before the king are dwarfed by the strong, strategic swimmer with the girth of a football and the length of a one-yard first down (three feet). The Chinook is sure in direction and conservative with resources. It doesn't dart, wave, or waste time. It advances efficiently within the water column from one step to the next, passing by one window, then the next, then out of sight. The shot is maybe five seconds. Maybe, but I have it. I drove all this way to get it. I knew they were moving. Historic timing records told me so. Now I have visual proof.

Salmon population counts start at Bonneville Dam. The reality is that we wouldn't know how many salmon there are—or aren't—without counting capabilities at dams, and what's on its way is first counted at Bonneville. The tally gets repeated at each wall. Scientists write numbers, and visitors witness the passing. With the dam closed, I'm today's only witness. In a small room somewhere in this cavern of man-made mechanics in the middle of nature's invention, a scientist is adding one more click to the total.

What's in the window survived the ocean. I'm on the right track, and it's officially verified by a flash sighting, but a sighting, nonetheless. Chinook salmon heading to Idaho have 704 miles to go. There's a reason my sighting is so fleeting. Salmon have no time, or energy, for darting and waving.

# SCAFFOLD

THERE'S ANOTHER SET of walls five miles from Bonneville Dam, Cascade Locks Marine Park. These walls are older and out of commission. Locks are built in rivers used for mass transit. This is the navigation purpose of dammed systems: boats, from barge to sail, enter lock lanes and stand by as water levels are lowered or raised to send them on their way with an appropriate amount of flow for their load. The locks at Cascade pushed steamboats up and down the Columbia River in the late 1800s before Bonneville Dam was built. Bonneville has locks so Cascade is no longer used for that purpose, but it's still plenty crowded in June.

When the fish run, the fishermen run to the locks. They stack themselves sardine style, barely a tackle box apart, along the cement walls of the old lock site. It's a crowd of masked and unmasked in close quarters. Driving through Oregon, I've seen "fake virus" spray painted on overpasses, and it's clear that not everyone heeds the warnings to stay apart. Catching fish for food and for fun won't be denied.

When I arrive at the locks, looking for Terrie Brigham, I find her easily—not in the casting crowd but on a scaffold. Terrie is from the Umatilla Native American tribe, who traditionally inhabited the Columbia plateau region. I found her through the Columbia River Inter-Tribal Fish Commission (CRITFC), which represents four tribes: Yakima, Umatilla, Warm Springs, and Nez Perce. When you want to interview a dam operator, you call the U.S. Army Corps of Engineers. When you want to interview a tribal fisher, you call CRITFC.

The commission fields your intentions and, if deemed prudent, finds a member willing to talk to the media. I could have taken my chances and tried approaching a tribal fisher at random while on the road, but that's too risky for how far I'm driving. I need a guarantee—a sure voice, a voice willing to talk with me, the white girl with media credentials.

Many tribal members are leery of two words in that description. *White* and *media*. Both have tainted Native truths throughout history. I don't want to do that. I have no problem explaining my intentions, my ignorance, and my desire to represent truths.

I'm constantly aware of the girl sandwiched between "white" and "media". My gender makes me a minority in the outdoor industry of which 95 percent of my stories come from. Men, particularly sportsmen, dominate the kind of assignments I cover. I'm also aware of my media status. Press isn't always welcome. If I'm unwelcome at the scene of a story it's for one of two reasons: because I'm media, or because I'm female. I can usually tell right away from someone's reaction which aspect of my identity is causing the discomfort, and often I know how to navigate it. Either I have to be okay with being unwelcome in many places I insert myself into, or I have to stop doing my job, or stop being female. I'm not interested in those last two options.

Of the three descriptors in "white girl with media credentials," white is the one I'm least aware of. I don't consider my actions or my attitude to be motivated by my skin color any more than I think someone else's skin color dictates their actions or attitude. Jerks are jerks. They come in all colors. So do kind people.

The tribal commission acknowledged the sincerity behind my intentions to include Native perspective in the story of salmon, and they found me a tribal voice. That voice belongs to Terrie. She helps manage her family's store, Brigham Fish Market, in the city of Cascade Locks. She grew up fishing with her aunties, and she's teaching her own kids how to fish.

Her scaffold, a flat deck of weathered wood with a ladder and a bucket, is attached to an expired lock lane. Her ancestors built it. Her family fishes from it. They're the only people who can use it.

Terrie's in muck boots, jeans, and a purple T-shirt, with her dark brown hair knotted atop her head. She doesn't see me unload my gear, so I don't introduce myself yet. She's not looking up, and she won't hear me over the cascade anyway. I'm watching her from above because the parking lot is positioned higher than her scaffold. Looking over the wall, she's about twenty feet below me. I'm going to have a lot of useless topknot shots if I don't find a better angle. I know I can't ask for an exception to the outsiders-not-allowed-on-scaffold policy just so I can get a better angle. I'll find a different shot without asking Terrie to compromise for me.

I notice that she's dipnetting, a tribal fishing technique. She has one hand on the handle of a net twice her height. The other hand holds string that's baited on the other end and bouncing in the current. Once she feels the string yank, she'll yank the handle. A large hoop netted for scooping will rise, hopefully with three to five fish at a time. The difference between a fish hitting the net and a fish taking the bait is subtle. She knows the difference. Her posture is stiff and alert. She's so still, her eyes could be closed behind her sunglasses, and I wouldn't know it, but there's no way they are. She's near the edge of the platform, five feet above water moving so fast it blurs under her boots. The push of that flow against the pole in her hand is a serious strain, but she's steady. Forget the take. I'd be flipped into the rapids on the first slight hit of a fish.

Ten seconds pass. Two minutes. She hasn't looked up. I'm still looking down, gripping the wall in anticipation. The hit happens in the next tick, and she turns it into a take by yanking up the pole hand over hand. It's my first look at a handmade dipnet, the tool that's fed her family for generations. It's full of shad.

"I've been on a scaffold since I was about eight years old," Terrie says, after transferring fish from net to bucket and climbing up the ladder to meet me. "You're not going to get rich doing this. You're going to get by."

Terrie sold spring Chinook for eight dollars a pound a decade ago. A decent margin, but that margin went downhill with the salmon population, so these days she supplements her income with shad. Shad are oily, loaf-sized fish. They're the fish I saw darting past the windows in high numbers. Terrie sells them from the cooler at the top of her ladder. Her son, Elliot, helps. He lowers a rope holding a white plastic bucket down the wall to his mom on the scaffold. Terrie transfers shad from the net to the bucket. Elliot pulls the rope, bringing the bucket up to parking lot level to be sold from the cooler in the back of Terrie's truck.

"Sometimes when you fish, it seems fun," Elliot says. "But sometimes it's not."

Elliot's in mucks, jeans, and T-shirt too. He's ten and his smile gaps where a few baby teeth haven't been replaced with permanent teeth yet. When I change angles by crossing to the other side of the lock for a wide shot rather than a top-knot shot, I capture his animation.

While he waits for the bucket to fill so he can pull it up, he sings. There's so much whitewater noise between us that I can't hear him, but I can tell he's singing. He forms his lips with such perfect exaggeration on each syllable that I can almost make out the words. He's jigging a bit, too, working his feet and forearms in and out like those mini-dance memes teens like to post on social media apps.

Amy's daughter, a teen bored of home school and pandemic life, is a few grades ahead of Elliot. She needed to get out so her mom brought her along when I was at Bonneville Dam. While she waited masked and at a distance for my tour to wrap, I saw her move farther from the group and entertain herself with steps like what Elliot is doing now. We're all rock stars on the inside. Or dancing queens. Or a combination of both on our best days when we think no one is watching. I like being that no one in those moments, catching people who assume they're unobserved.

As the shy little girl with long brown hair—long enough to hide my eyes—I always looked away when others looked at me. And when someone looked away in response, I looked back. I watched people and they didn't know it. I still watch. And others still don't know it. I'm not invading privacy—I'm invading the personal sphere. Not so personal that someone's hiding and I'm seeking, but personal enough for them to show me their soul, and I'm astute enough to know that's what's happening because I do the same thing. Rock, my star, and dance, my queen.

I watch Elliot finish his lip-sync-groove routine, then approach to ask him if he likes to eat fish. With kids, your questions must move beyond yes or no answers by starting with why. Most kids won't elaborate on their own, but you need more than yes/no answers to tell a story on screen. So instead of "Do you like to eat fish?" I ask, "Why do you like to eat fish?" Why questions require more than yes or no. Whys motivate kids to talk. So does asking about their favorites. "What's your favorite part of the fish to eat?"

"The tail," Elliot says.

He says tail without hesitation, but describing what tail tastes like is hard for him. He stops midsentence, taps his chin, and rolls his eyes to the sky, searching the mist for the right words. He knows I'm watching and yet his innate animation is still on full display. His personality must be enhanced with humor.

He knows the taste of tail texture but doesn't know how to talk through it. I gather he likes to eat the tail because it's crunchy, kind of like potato chips. He tells me that's close to what he means and keeps sorting shad from his family's cooler in the truck bed to a customer's cooler on the sidewalk.

Within the salmon run, Terrie catches one blueback, a nickname for sockeye salmon. She can't sell sockeye because the commercial salmon fishing season is closed. There weren't enough clicks on the tally chart at the dam, but as a tribal member, she can keep it. It goes in a different cooler for dinner later. Elliot has already claimed the tail.

# WIND

THE SCAFFOLD IS empty in the channel below John Day Lock and Dam. The wind is so strong, I'm amazed any scaffold stays tethered to the side of the channel for one season, let alone the several seasons it's endured. Ladders are removed when scaffolds aren't occupied, so there's no way for the uninvited to stand on one. Ladders or not, I wouldn't venture. I know that sacred, traditional stage is not mine. It's the tribe's.

There were tribal fishers at The Dalles Lock and Dam between Bonneville and John Day, but I didn't talk to any of them. I shot footage of the dam and let them be. The Dalles is a place many Native Americans won't visit. They stopped spending time at The Dalles when the site they'd known as Celilo Falls was waterlogged by dam construction in 1957. Celilo Falls, the oldest continuously inhabited community on the North American continent until its destruction, had been an important place for tribes—and it still is—but they can't see it anymore. The generations-steeped Indian salmon fishery is now underwater, the falls turned flat, proving there was more than natural resource at stake when the dams were built. Natural heritage sunk too.

The Dalles is mile 191 of 850. John Day is mile 215 of 850. There are scaffolds at John Day, but no one is fishing. It provides another bleak peek at our planet without people. Like the desolate beach I saw at the mouth of the Columbia, the pandemic often puts scenes void of people in your face. Besides, the is wind too strong for scaffold stance. It's too strong for my 125-pound frame.

I'm parked in the middle of a dirt lot downstream of the dam. The gusts are more than twenty miles an hour, so the bushes bend away from the wind and toward the water. The few trees around assume the same hunched posture. The only thing not leaning toward the water is the water itself, and that's because the spray squeezed through the dam takes a hard right as soon as it shoots out, the wind instantly carrying the rushing mist to the bank across the river from me.

I angle my truck broadside to the bully of a breeze, creating a wind break to reduce camera shake. Around the Dalles, the second dam out of eight, the scenery turned from rainforest to desert, so I'm dry and relatively warm. John Day is the third dam. McNary is the fourth. Both are easily accessible off the highway on the Columbia River and still in Oregon.

I'm shooting footage of John Day's midstream structure, solid and liquid in a head-on collision, when a helicopter enters my shot top left of frame. It's several hundred feet overhead. There's a basket cabled below the chopper, similar to the baskets tethered to hot air balloons. Two bodies are in the basket. I pan to the right, following the cargo, to see that it's a pair of men holding an orange-red ball the size of Jupiter leaning out of the basket as soon as the propellers hold in hover stance.

The men are attaching the ball to a powerline longer than the width of the dam, which is more than twenty football fields wide bank to bank. Their method reminds me of bait fisherman attaching bobbers to fishing line, but on a ginormous scale. Wind be damned; it's maintenance day for the power company.

When you visit a dam, look at it, then look up. Power lines web high over the water. At the conversion of man and Mother Nature, there's a massive amount of energy. Energy the Bonneville Power Administration (BPA) was invented for. BPA lights up the Pacific Northwest with electricity generated primarily by water, the Columbia River Basin its source.

"Nothing happens without electricity," says Doug Johnson, Bonneville Power Administration spokesperson, when I interview him on a sunny (solar), windy (wind) day next to the river (hydro). "And public power has predominantly been the engine that has made this region work."

Public power used by utilities in the Pacific Northwest is predominantly clean, renewable hydropower, and because it's public, it's funded by consumers like you and me. We pay a fee every time we flip a switch. The watts that keep our world rotating are fairly cheap in the Pacific Northwest, but they are not free. Nearly 30 percent of ratepayers in the Pacific Northwest light up their life with power provided by BPA. A portion of every power bill goes back to the supplying source, which is water, and the wildlife living in that water. We've spent an estimated eighteen billion dollars on salmon and steelhead recovery in the last thirty years, since about the time several species warranted threatened and endangered listing. Those billions come from our own wallets every time we leave the lights on.

I live in Idaho Falls, Idaho. My house is warm, my fridge is cool, my computer works, and my porch is lit. Those things happen because I pay my monthly power bill. I'm an Idaho Falls Power customer, a city-owned utility that's part of the BPA grid. BPA must mitigate for damage done to natural resources, mostly salmon, because of the dams, so thirteen cents of every one dollar I pay goes to fish and wildlife recovery efforts funded by BPA—but really it's funded by you and me.

In one month, my household of four uses 617 kilowatts, costing us thirty-nine dollars with five dollars of that allocated to salmon recovery. Multiply that by twelve months for twenty years, and I see that I've paid twelve hundred dollars to help save fish trying to navigate dams that generate power for my daily living. I've paid it, and you've paid it.

When we pay for hydropower, we're paying for flow. Flowing water turns undersurface machines, or turbines. That spinning action creates electricity sent to power lines originating at the dam site. Those lines tentacle across the country lightning fast, like veins pumping your blood, so that when you turn on your TV, there's instant picture. That's hydropower. Throwing water directly on a socket is a terrible idea, but when it pushes through a series of engineering wonders, it works. The Columbia River Basin is a workhorse for power. John Day Dam is part of the eight-workhorse team.

I watch the well-orchestrated circus in the sky. The basket and its aerial motor shift back and forth. Land, lift. More balls sit on the bank, each ready to be attached during its own flight mission. The linemen are wrangling in the wind just fine, but I have a hot mess on the ground. An airstream grabs my hat. When I instinctively reach for it, a gust grabs my camera and dumps it in the dirt. Three pieces of equipment roll toward the scaffold shuffling to the cliff's edge, buoyed by wind. I'll never get the pieces if they go over the edge. Thankfully, they stop at the rocks.

The front of my camera has separated from its body. My lens hood, polarized filter, and focus ring are broken. I throw a fit. I would have rolled in the dirt and kicked if I knew I could bath later, but I don't have a tub, so I stomp around collecting bits, knowing there's no repair service out here. No rush or overnight shipping to the river or anywhere else during a pandemic. This camera is made in China and shipping anything from the origin of the pandemic is problematic. I don't have replacement money, anyway. I'm screwed.

All accounted for, I have five cameras. My primary camera—the one worth thousands of dollars that shoots every interview plus anything that isn't aerial or underwater—is busted. I throw the pieces in the backseat of my truck and stomp around some more before I figure out a fix. Damn the dam and its wind. My grizzly bear hat is my lucky hat. Of course I'm going to reach for it when it leaves my head. It's not my lucky hat anymore. Maybe I should tape it on my head. That's it! Tape.

I add a layer of silver duct tape to the bottom of every new video camera as soon as I take it out of the box. It reduces dings and adds a thin buffer strip to the body. I have to set my camera down in a lot of less than ideal places. On long road trips like this, I carry a tool bag holding many survival items, including red duct tape. I secure mic cables to floors with it to reduce trips.

I find the tape and stick the camera pieces where they should be using tape to puzzle the pieces into place around the lens. Then I wrap more tape around the whole front end like the fists of a boxer. It will hold. The lens is protected, but I won't be able to focus manually, as I've lost access to the focus ring under the tape. I'll have to rely on auto focus for the rest of the summer. I'm at mile 215 of 850, which means I'll have to shoot more than half of this migration with a broken camera. That's the last thing I want to do, but that's what I must do when working with the impossible during a pandemic.

# PART II:

## Snake River

# GRAPES

IT'S MOVING DAY. I'm changing rivers and changing states, done on the Columbia River in Oregon. I'm starting on the Snake River in Washington at the beginning of week two on the road. I overnighted on a bluff upstream of Ice Harbor Lock and Dam, the first of four dams on the Snake, 334 miles from the Pacific Ocean.

I parked at the end of a dirt road with my camper door facing east, so the sun is my alarm clock. Summer means more day than night, which also means more shooting light. I rise early, trained by personal and professional ritual. The best light arrives early and leaves late.

When light enters the skinny rectangle door of my camper, I know it's time to run. Today I'm running through early light instead of recording it. I've sat for so many days in drive mode that my joints and rod are cramped. I need to run before I work.

I like running at sunrise, especially if I'm running somewhere new, and this morning I'm somewhere I've never been before. It's a vineyard near Pasco, Washington. I stick my feet in my trail running shoes and tie them while sitting on the steps of my camper. I stand, zip my mint green jacket to my chin, and put my sunglasses on my sun-screened face. I head west with the sun at my back. Alfalfa grows in the field on my right, a pivot with its turn in the water rights rotation sprinkling green heads that haven't matured yet. Harvest is a ways off still.

On my left, more green sprawls out before me. Grapes. The watering can for these vines is dripline, like a soaker hose, rather than pivot sprinkler that rotates on wheels over alfalfa. Fields on both sides of me are drinking. I can smell it. It's the damp in the desert. Moist ground has a scent, like rain-infused soil left to breathe in a cellar. Although the crops I alley through vary, their source of growth is the same. Their hose is the Snake River, more specifically the pool behind Ice Harbor Dam at the bottom of the bluff I'm running on. It takes a lot of power to pump water to high ground in southeastern Washington, but here it is. Lush acres with parched, unfarmed parcels mere acres away.

"Anything that you see up and down this stretch of the river that's green is green because it's being watered with river water," says Katie Nelson, Gordon Estate Winery general manager. "It's everything for us and for any farmers in our area. None of the farms around us would be here if we didn't irrigate. If we go one year without water, we're done."

Katie manages a family business her dad and uncle started in the early 1980s. Back then, grapes weren't a commodity in Washington, but with conditions similar to wine country in France, her dad, Jeff, thought, why not? He bought acreage on the bluff with water rights to the river below and planted vines worthy of harvest. The Gordons grow grapes you can drink.

I don't know how to make wine, but I know how to drink wine, and drink it I do. I prefer reds over whites, blends over cabs, Italian over Spanish, and flavor over price. Wine is a satisfying sensory game for me because I have an over-active palate—not an official diagnosis but a self-diagnosis. An over-active palate is a real drawback around rancid recipes but a bonus among the well prepared, and wine is most often well prepared. I can have one sip of red wine and tell you whether it contains chocolate or cherries. Fun party trick like the guy who always shows off by shotgunning beer.

The pandemic encourages many fears, and my biggest is losing my palate. I enjoy tasting food and drink like I enjoy smelling fresh air. Tasting is part of my eating experience, quite possibly the only part of my experience or in equal part with smelling. Blindfold me and I'll still enjoy eating and be able tell you what we're having without seeing it.

One of the most common COVID-19 symptoms is loss of taste or smell or both. To me, losing the ability to taste would be like losing fresh air, only I'd starve under one circumstance and suffocate under the other.

I do neither as I run the rows, feasting with my eyes and breathing with my lungs. Running where wine grows is invigorating. Sprouts of potential spread across orderly grow posts that are only head high. From my vantage point, I don't feel buried in the field. I can see over the crown of the plants, especially at the rise of every rolling hill. It's all so tidy. Wave after wave of straight vine lines unfurling like a flag in soft breeze all the way to the edge of the bluff. Beyond that, the cobalt coupling of sky and Snake. A barge is heading upstream. It must have passed through the lock at the dam earlier this morning. Also heading upstream, but next to the water instead of in it, is a lengthy, one-hundred-car train. I still count train cars as they pass like I did when I was little, multiplying the count by two for double stackers.

The track carves so close to the edge of the opposite bluff, I imagine a slight tip sending the train car-by-car into the river below, then sinking to the bottom while the barge keeps going. Both modes of traffic are common in the basin. What's not common is the cargo on the barge. It's not crops but blades.

I live on the same river as Katie: the Snake. We are separated by hundreds of miles, but what's passing Katie's house is barging toward my house. The water moving the blades produces hydropower at the dam that keeps the barge en route. The barge, which needs dams to move, shuttles the blades a wind turbine needs to produce power. If enough blades are shuttled by barge, then one day we might not need the hydropower produced at dams. We might not need the dams at all, and then what would the barges do? The barge quite possibly transports something that could someday make itself obsolete. I stare at the ironic shipment for so long that my running heart rate drops to sitting rate, so I walk one row before picking up the pace on the next.

It's too early in the season for grapes to weigh heavy, causing the branches to droop a bit so the leaves freely wiggle some in the light wind. They're popping with emerald optimism, enjoying the secured supply of the new dripline. It improves water efficiency, which, in the desert, is the holy grail. How best to use limited water for unlimited future.

The vineyard I'm running through is the future of the Gordon family, and lucky for us, we can drink their future bottled as reds and whites. Katie needs clean air, clean earth, and clean water to stay in business. Even spent seeds have a purpose at her place. That's what's under my feet. It's so curious to me that I have to stop, crouch, and scoop to be sure. Yep, it's spent grape seed. The cinder-colored specks of harvests past cover dirt roads to keep the dust down. The sensation on my soles feels strange when I run. It's crunchy cushion underfoot as I work the kinks free so I can get back to work.

Just like Katie, I need clean air, clean earth, and clean water to do my job. I've covered outdoor and environment stories for more than two decades, but really it's people I've covered. I tell the stories of our planet through the voices of the people who protect it and the people who exploit it. But let it also be said that just because the good intentions of one person don't match the good intentions of another doesn't mean one or the other is bad. They're just different. Differences, when mingled in the right doses, make miracles.

Sometimes opposition mixes like an Easter egg dipped in two contrasting cups of dye. Half red, half yellow, orange where they meet. The narrow band of orange has to turn into the sweet spot for salmon, the miracle. Ironically, it's also the color of the fish's flesh when we fillet it for dinner. Red doesn't want to be yellow and vice versa, but can they find common ground. When they do, there are possibilities we haven't thought of yet.

Katie considers herself environmentally conscious; she has to be to work the land. It won't provide if she neglects it. Changing to dripline is a water conservation measure Katie is proud of. Figuring out how to pump water from a pool in the river to the crops in her field above is another feat she protects. But that pool is made by a dam in a river salmon need. She's interested in conserving water. She's not interested in removing the dam.

I run a short but hilly three miles, then circle back to my house on wheels. I return to find a bottle of red wine and a bag of cherries on my camper steps. Katie's husband, Marc, is in charge of cherry harvest. Beyond the vines there are acres of fruit trees full of ladders, barrels, and pickers harvesting yet another crop grown with the same water that grows fish.

I breakfast on cherries, spit bath to conceal sweat, change clothes to freshen up, and find Katie in the winery on the other end of the vineyard. She's shipping bottles since their new storefront in Kennewick had to close as soon as it opened because of the pandemic. Terrible timing, but the grapes are still growing, so she's shipping orders instead.

Every business in retail is shipping its products. Humans try to resist change, but they really do know how to adapt when a situation turns desperate. Besides cleaning companies, the other business to be in during a pandemic is shipping. Katie's grapes will grow, crush, ferment, and ship unfazed by the virus hanging over us. She's optimistic about vine volume but worries about water. She bristles when I ask her about removing dams to recover salmon. She's not anti-salmon. She's pro-dam.

"Dams are just not something that you can take away," Katie says while gingerly adding bottles to a shipping box. "It's like . . . you can't put the toothpaste back in the tube."

I admire Katie's courage. She not afraid to talk in blunt terms about sensitive subjects. She's afraid of what she'll lose if saving salmon becomes more important than sustaining her family's business. I lost more than half of my business when I broke my leg because I couldn't walk. I can't imagine losing all of my business because I can't water my crops. I don't want to lose salmon, and I don't want Katie to lose her farm.

Katie's crop is her family's livelihood. They have a crop because they have water rights. They have water rights because a pump sucks river uphill. There's river downhill because that's where the Snake River is. The Snake stores water because there's a wall in the river—Ice Harbor Dam. Gordon Estate Winery's irrigation water is in the pool behind the dam. If the dam goes away, the pool goes away. Losing a farm for a fish is a big ask.

If the dams are breeched and the pools drop, the same brains that built dams and pumped water to higher ground will have to figure out how to satisfy Katie's water rights with longer hoses and stronger pumps. Figure that out and common ground, that orange band, may a miracle make. It's farms *and* fish rather than farms or fish. Just like career *and* kids, the goal has to be both, not either.

# GAG

THE NOISE TENDS to ease up when I switch rivers and cross the Oregon-Washington border. The volume change isn't because there's less traffic, but because there's less people. The Oregon side of the Columbia River is urban. The Snake River in Washington is rural. There's less development along the ribs of the river in Washington, but more movement through the middle. What's grown must get to the coast, and the most cost effective way to get it there is by river rather than by road.

Much of where the Snake ribbons through Washington is remote, undeveloped brown foothills tucked out of the way. Dam sites, especially during the pandemic when access is closed, are one-way ventures. The road requires visitors to go out the same way they came in by doubling back on a two-lane pave that requires them to drive nearly six times more miles than the fish swim.

As I drive along, I see the Snake in fits and spits in Washington, unlike the constant ripple of reveal the Columbia offers along the highway in Oregon. I have to go out of my way to see the Snake. It carves harsh, deep canyons and eases up soft hillsides, but far fewer people see what the Snake does because it isn't easy to get to.

The one planning error I make on this multi-state adventure bites me on the Snake. I slotted one day to see four dams: Ice Harbor, Lower Monumental, Little Goose, and Lower Granite. They're spread between river mile 334 and 432 of 850. That's four stops in less than one hundred river miles, but I'm not on the river. I'm on the road, and I've lost track of how many more miles that makes this stretch of the trip. My plan was to transition from grapes to grain in one day while seeing the Snake and its four dams.

On a map it looked doable. After easily driving four dams on the Columbia in four days—Bonneville, Dalles, John Day, and McNary—another four dams in one day seemed reasonable, but by the second of the Snake's four, I know I'm wrong. Don't try to see all four Lower Snake River Dams in one day if you want to be there for more than a blink. That's what I had to do to keep the rest of my shoots on schedule for the rest of the week.

It took me twelve hours of no-messing-around driving to see four dams in one day. They're so way back in there, boat may have been faster because of the massive difference between river miles and road miles. It's like saying, "as the crow flies" when you can't fly and must hike up hill and down dell ten times to reach the ridgeline the crow flies directly to. As the river flows, the road doesn't always go.

I rationed my onsite time to ten minutes at each dam. That turns into thirteen minutes at Little Goose Lock and Dam because of one pelican. I see a pelican, and I gag. I'm lab-rat trained to bend over and roll my guts to my gullet when I see American white pelicans. The pelican at Little Goose hunts while I heave, my over-active palate on overload. The puke reaction comes from an assignment a few years ago on Gull Island, also known by me as Gag Island. My Gull Island story was a one-time deal with a lasting impression.

There were gulls on the patch of ground in the middle of Idaho's Blackfoot Reservoir—egrets, too, but pelicans outnumber everything else during nesting season. The adults are big. Their babies are big but can't fly, and pelicans of all ages panic when corralled, which turns into a puke fest.

The sunrise the morning I arrived by boat at the island was spectacular, but I didn't care. I didn't want to look around, but I did want to stop breathing. I'd never wanted to stop breathing, but at that moment, the urge overwhelmed me. I'd bent over on the bank with my equipment at my feet and my backpack off so that when I leaned over I wouldn't tip over.

"Get a grip, lady," I said, issuing my own pep talk. "You're a professional. You've smelled worse." Sniff. Gag. Cover mouth. "No I haven't."

I straightened, trying to inhale air through my mouth instead of my nostrils. I swallowed bugs then had to spit. I gave my nose another shot at its job with a tiny test whiff. The stink sickened me again. I'd been warned about the rank smell of a pelican colony. The warning wasn't nearly strong enough.

"It's horrible," said pelican bander Dan Seymour as he handed me a blue facemask. "Absolutely horrible. You don't know what you're getting into until you come here."

I came to shoot a story about one of the few pelican colonies in Idaho. The giant birds' nest on Gull Island every summer, and Idaho Department of Fish and Game bands and tags three hundred chicks before they leave the nest. The pelicans were only a few months old but close to the adult size of twenty pounds but with no flight capabilities yet. They piled on top of each other like sheep that wouldn't separate. They snapped their long beaks in defense. The frenzy stirred up a sensory assault of wet feces, spent feathers, and regurgitated fish. When pelicans panic, they puke. What they throw up is what they eat. Fish.

"The smell definitely rings your bell at first," Dan said. "We're stepping not only on dirt but years and years of grossness. Definitely wear boots. You are not going to want to come out here wearing flip flops."

I hid my gags behind the mask and started shooting photos and video. The smell was still too much, but the island had tremendous avian appeal. I scanned with my lens and found endless framing options. Feathers were everywhere. Pelicans, egrets, cormorants, herons, and gulls. Their calls mixed in a ruckus that assaulted my ears almost as much as the smell did. The birds lifted and landed with wings of white, gray, and black. I could barely keep my shots in focus. I finished recording free birds and turned to the trapped. There was a corral of orange netting holding pelicans, the hub of the stench fest. When biologists enter the corral, the grab and tag is on. One gloved hand goes around the beak. The other hand wraps around the wings and slides under the belly.

"You can't be hesitant. No. Absolutely not. They will gang up on you," Dan said with a pelican tucked under his arm. Dan's a redheaded fish technician sporting jokes and smiles. He made the disgusting laughable joke: "Go for the beak first and once you got it, grab them and go for it, but watch out for their buddies because they'll get you."

I felt like they'd all gotten me as I gagged again. The only thing the mask did was hide my gag, not reduce it. I could feel my hideous facial contortions mid-gag, so the mask saved me some dignity. This trip took place long before we fought over wearing masks. This mask was issued to keep people from inhaling pelican production, not the viral germs of other people. We had no idea what would be coming for us. Had I known, I would have kept that mask. They're sold out now.

Armloads of birds are tagged for tracking purposes because they don't stay on Gull Island. They nest then leave for places as far away as Kansas and Canada. While nesting, pelicans eat up to five pounds of fish a day, some of which are Yellowstone cut-throat trout—natives just like salmon. The cuttie population is struggling, but so are pelicans. Biologists need to know where the birds go before they do anything about the ones nesting on the island. Reducing the pelican population on Gull Island to protect cutthroat trout may knock out a pelican colony some-where else.

"Whenever you have one species impacting another, it's always a balancing act," said Colleen Moulton, Idaho Department of Fish and Game avian ecologist as she clipped a numbered tag to a pelican wing. "You try to figure out what the best balance is to make sure you are preserving both species and making sure one isn't having too much of an impact on the other."

Colleen didn't wear a mask and didn't gag. She thought pelicans were pretty. I thought she was off-kilter, but I was fas-cinated by her tolerance. Maybe her sense of smell was blocked since birth, long before COVID-19 could steal it.

Banding three hundred pelicans took a full day. It was well past lunchtime, and I was well past hungry, but I was still wearing the mask. There was no way I could stomach the smell long enough to take off the mask and eat. The sensory assault continued to overwhelm me, but I managed to take in the wonder that only a mass concentration of birds can offer, and I realized that's part of the attraction for those willing to wrangle pelicans in panic mode.

With my pelican auto-response revisited for three minutes at Little Goose, I gather myself and my gear and give the scene ten minutes of shooting time. Dam in the background, puke-inducing pelican in the foreground. The bird isn't bothered by me as it bobs along the foam line, scooping small fish into its beaked pocket that's as soft as brushed leather. I know what's in that pouch. I've seen it, smelled it. Those black dots on that butter smooth food pouch are lice. Lice, I tell you. That's what bird biologists told me when I finally figured out how to tuck and run with a pelican that needed a tag. Dan had tried to calm my hysterics.

"If lice gets on you, don't worry," He'd said. "It can only survive on you for two days."

Two days. Are you kidding me? Gross. The pelican at Little Goose has blue eyes. I dare not say pretty, but they're pretty blue. I wonder if it's already eaten five pounds of young salmon today. That's why it's here. The bird knows food comes out of the pipe downstream of the dam. The pop gun and sprinkler spray may bug circling gulls, but the big white bird floats leisurely out of hazing range, eating the day away. It sits high in the water, buoyant from the little air bags in its chest that feel like packing peanuts when you palm its underside.

I don't have the luxury of leisure. I'm short on time, and this rotten flashback isn't helping. Stop staring at the stinkin' bird, I tell myself. Grab soda crackers out of the camper. Get in the truck. Drive to the next dam.

The sites are closed with no one around, so I have no delays, besides pelicans, and no one in my way. But even without traffic, I barely make it to my next D&D before dark. Cell coverage doesn't reach far in these parts, so electronic navigation is unreliable. I work in a lot of places where that happens, so I carry an atlas. Like the red duct tape repairing my camera in a pinch, the soft-side book of roads by state filed between my passenger seat and console comes in handy. I have to stop about every hour to study it. I must be sure I'm on the right road because there's no extra time for a wrong turn.

I drive fast. I stop for gas once at a pump in the middle of nowhere. No convenience store, no repair shop, just a pump. I race past the one pump, then turn around. Just like carrying an atlas for going off-grid and having a mask for pelicans and pandemics, I know better. If you see no-frills fuel offering nothing but hose and magnetic strip for swiping your card, you always stop. Never pass. Stop. One pump means there's no other fuel for a long ways, and a lot of other people ran out of gas right here before this pump was put in.

# GRANITE

DAMS ARE ONE of the most historic, hot-button issues in our nation. They have been for a century. The first arguments were about building dams. Today, it's about knocking them down. There's no doubt dams developed the West. They drastically changed watersheds in the West too. Undoing what's done suggests nothing short of taking drastic action once again.

There are dozens of dams in the Columbia River Basin, and dozens of salmon runs are impacted by those dams, but for Chinook swimming to the Yankee Fork, there are eight major pinch points: Four dams on the Columbia River in Oregon and four dams on the Snake River in Washington. The string of eight ends at Lower Granite Lock and Dam in Pomeroy, Washington. It's near the Idaho border, 432 miles from the Pacific Ocean. Returning salmon are considered Idaho-bound if they make it past Lower Granite.

I meet Keith Petersen past Lower Granite. His dad helped build Bonneville Dam. He grew up in Washington, then served as Idaho's state historian until he retired in 2015. He

stands at the windows in the walls often, and he's navigated the
Columbia River Basin by barge once. That excursion happened
when he wrote *River of Life, Channel of Death: Fish and Dams
on the Lower Snake* in 1995.

I was in college studying to be a professional communicator
when Keith was researching the route I'm on now. When I'm
studying an area, I want to know its natural resources. When
Keith studies an area, he wants to know its history.

"I'm not sure that America is ready for the extinction of
salmon," he says, as we stand on a dock tacked to the Snake
River. "But it's a very complicated issue when you ask, 'Are fish
worth so much that we're willing to take down dams?'"

His perspective on salmon recovery is valuable because he
knows how to translate where our nation was when the walls
went up, when the West became an economic force to be reck-
oned with because of hydropower and hydro highway.

"Dams were amazing things," Keith says. "They were
things that you wanted to go visit. You wanted to see them."

Keith, with a graying beard and caring eyes rimmed by
round glass, knows that dam passage is a problem for fish.
He also knows, based on historical records, that dam builders
knew it would be a problem for fish, but society had bigger
problems that could be fixed with dams. So four went up, then
another four.

"I think most people, like my family, didn't really see the
conflict between fish and dams," Keith says, when we continue
our interview after two wave runners spin donuts in the bay by
the dock, the recreation aspect of pools behind dams. "Those
stories of salmon and dams were just part of what I grew up
with. The two of them together."

Lower Granite, completed in 1984, is an Idaho-bound salmon's proverbial white flag on the racetrack. A white flag signals the final lap, the last push before a checkered flag finish. Passing Lower Granite warrants a white flag. Those fish are entering their final lap. Passage doesn't guarantee migration completion or spawn success, but odds improve significantly for Chinook passing Lower Granite. After that, they're dam free, headed to and through Idaho's Salmon River corridor. Running 425 miles, it's one of the longest undammed rivers in the nation.

There are more than four dams on the whole Snake, so the four in question are often called the Lower Snake River dams since they're in the last section of the Snake that dumps into the Columbia. For fish on their way home, these four are the last four of eight. When anti-dam parties say, "Free the Snake," they're referring to removal of these four Lower Snake dams: Ice Harbor, Lower Monumental, Little Goose, and Lower Granite.

There's no guarantee freeing the Snake will save salmon, but the arguments for it are persuasive. And so are the arguments against it, which is why the dams still stand.

Freeing the Snake isn't a one-sided discussion. It's not a two-sider either. Not us versus them, farm versus fish, or power versus play. There are many priorities and perspectives. All of them matter more than picking a side. Most people want salmon to persist—it's *how* they'll persist that raises hackles.

This is the light bulb moment right here. The four Lower Snake River dams produce a thousand megawatts of hydropower, enough to light up Seattle. It takes 1,428 wind turbines to generate the same amount of power if the breeze is consistent. It isn't, but river consistently streams through the basin all day every day. Say dams are easy to remove, though they're not. Say power is easy to replace, though it's not. Both are doable, but not easy. In a world where those sticking points are unstuck, what's the problem? The problem isn't fuses. It's farms.

Breeching dams drops pool levels behind dams. If we lower the water level, we leave irrigators, like Katie at Gordon Estate Winery,  holding rights to a dry tap. More than ninety thousand acres of crops—food—feed off those pools in Washington. It would cost an estimated $622 million to adjust irrigation structures if the pumps don't reach the pools because the dams aren't holding back water anymore.

Beyond irrigation, there's transportation to consider. Dams make commodities, power, and dams move commodities, crops. Barges loaded with grain won't budge without dams. Manipulating flow through pools and locks is what moves boat traffic in the basin. To replace one grain barge, you need 134 semitrucks or 35 train cars and a whole lot of new road and rail space for both.

Not everyone thinks dams are the demise of fish, and they don't want to see their own demise to find out if they are. That's why unison is ever out of reach. Throw in the challenges that come from harvest, habitat, and hatcheries with hydropower too. The debate is layered, but on paper it looks flat. It shouldn't be translated by one person—me, the writer. Debates are not solo. Speeches are solo, and this isn't a speech. It's a change in story format for one chapter to encourage depth not found in paragraph form.

I'm visiting with people who have a stake in the Columbia River Basin, a basin that hosts threatened and endangered fish and used to host other fish that are now extinct. They're giving me their take on the dam debate as I migrate with salmon from the ocean to Idaho, seeking to understand a complex issue in simple terms. I ask the same question during every interview.

Dams. Should they stay or should they go? The answer is never the same.

"I think they should go. Absolutely. 100 percent. The dams should go because the river was made to flow from headwaters to the ocean unimpeded. With dams in place, I do not see a way that our fish can return to the way they were and the way they should be."
-Kyle Jones, Jones Sport Fishing

"We've got to know a little more than I think we know right now to make that leap. Do you really want to take one thousand average megawatts of electricity, which is enough power to light up the city of Seattle, with the risk associated with abundance of fish?"
-Doug Johnson, Bonneville Power Administration

"You don't little bit breech a dam. You either do or you don't, and once you do, it's still an experiment."
-David Doeringsfeld, Port of Lewiston

"It's imperative that we talk about the four dams on the Lower Snake being the highest priority for breeching or removal. We have spent over thirty years trying every solution to recover Chinook salmon except dam breeching, and we have not gained any ground."
-Cassi Wood, Trout Unlimited

"The salmon are in the river. Granted they've had some pressure, but I can't see losing hydropower. It's as close to a no-brainer for society as I can think. The water is going to the ocean anyway—just capture some horse-power out of it, and there's a lot of people who don't realize Portland used to flood all the time before we had dams on the Snake and Columbia Rivers."
-Joseph Anderson, grain farmer

"These things need to stay because they're too import-ant to the economy. Yes, they might be harmful to an endangered species, but we need to figure out other things to help them because these need to stay."
-Katie Nelson, Gordon Estate Winery

"If the dams stay, I really think that's it. I think we need to make a decision whether we want salmon or those four Lower Snake dams. It's pretty obvious that that's just a slow play to extinction, and that's unacceptable."
-Lytle Denny, Shoshone-Bannock Tribes

# GRAIN

JOSEPH "JOE" ANDERSON, the guy with the no-brainer opinion, says without doubt, without hesitation, that the dams should stay. He's a grain grower in Lewiston, Idaho. It's the first major town after the chain of eight dams. Major is a relative term. At thirty-two thousand people, Lewiston is rural but considered a major town in the region because bedroom communities around it are smaller.

Joe doesn't need the Snake River for irrigation. He needs it for transportation. That's how he moves his crop to market. He barges his harvest to the coast via the Snake, plus the Columbia, with the help of dam flow control. He then uses the Pacific Ocean to move it overseas.

"Affordable transportation is one of the things that has helped the Northwest thrive," Joe says. "Without barge transportation, we drop below the cost of production, and we lose a lot of farmers."

Lewiston is a port town, the farthest inland seaport in the US. It's 465 miles from the Pacific Ocean. What ports out of this town is grain grown by Joe and many other families who farm the acreage sandwiched between the Clearwater River and the Snake River. Beyond that land, there's miles upon miles of otherwise undeveloped country. Much of the area is best seen by jetboat, which is why recreational traffic shares lanes with commercial shipments.

Soft white wheat grows prolifically in the area, and farmers knew they had something special to sell if they could just get it out of Lewiston so for decades, they pushed for a port that would provide direct access to the coast for shipping crops. The campaign started in 1931. The first barge left Lewiston in 1975.

"I probably can't make money right now without the port," Joe says.

When you want to talk to a farmer, you talk to them in their element. In a field. I covered crops and crime as reporter for a decade before I found my niche in outdoors and environment. I'm just as comfortable talking crops with a farmer as I am covering the case of a convicted felon in a court room—well, almost as comfortable.

That inmate serving time for a violent murder, trying to overturn his conviction, picked his nose every time I pointed my lens his direction in court. He shriveled my sense of comfort. I don't miss covering crime. And I don't miss covering crops, because I still cover crops. I can't live in an agriculturally dominated state like Idaho, with every drop of river allocated for irrigation, without covering crops and knowing how to talk to farmers in their fields.

I always meet growers on their ground when I have enough time to get there. They're in their element in that environment, more relaxed, more candid. Interviews in ag land are unfiltered.

When you meet them in their realm, farmers will lift the curtain on their expertise, and their opinions, with stern reasons for why they stand where they do. If you want raw and rural, get in the dirt.

The first farmer I ever talked to was Fred. I was twelve when I met Fred, so it was before I was a reporter. I grew up in Utah, west of the Wasatch Range. It was already urban back then, but a few farms still held rank around the rougher edges. Farmer Fred grew corn in those edges, and he paid a bushel of neighborhood kids peck-weight wages to hand-pick his corn, which he sold at corner stands around town.

I have no idea what his profit margins were, as I didn't even know what profit margins were back then. I just knew if you wanted to hang out with your friends in the summer, you had to work for Farmer Fred because everyone was in his fields. You had to be twelve to ride in the back of Farmer Fred's truck on corn-picking day, so the spring I turned twelve, I put myself on Farmer Fred's payroll for the summer.

I replaced a pair of gloves weekly, spending most of my salary on hand protection while also worrying about earwigs. I'm a lefty, so I always twisted cobs with my left arm, stacking them like cut wood in the curve of my right arm. I could hold up to twelve cobs at a time before I had to walk to row end and stash my cache in the flatbed trailer attached to Farmer Fred's truck.

With every cob twist, I leaned my body away from the shuck and my head far back from the stalk to avoid the earwigs that always shook loose. They'd land on my shoulder in haste, then try to weasel their way up to do what we all fear they do: wriggle into your brain through your ear hole, laying eggs as they go. Farmer Fred was taller than his crop—Utah corn doesn't grow nearly as tall as Nebraska corn—so he entered fields with no fear of earwigs.

While we pre-teens piled out of the truck bed, he chose a row. We'd stand at one end of a field that stretched a mile long, waiting. Picking our way through one row would take an hour, the ground under feet mud-wet, the stalks overhead dripping wet. Our shifts didn't start until Farmer Fred said so.

He'd walk a few paces within a row, looking for well irrigated corn, not the shrunken stuff suffering on the ends. We waited on the suffering end while he walked. Sometimes he'd walk so far in, we'd lose sight of him. He'd twist off a cob and walk back into eye sight and ear shot. He'd pull the bloody tissue out of his nostril, the dry country giving him nosebleeds, then put the cob in his mouth. Raw. He'd bite off a half-dozen kernels and smear another half-dozen kernels on his chin. He'd chew, taste, and swallow. If the taste was ripe, he'd put the blood plug back in his nose, drop the cob, and holler, "Start pickin'!"

We'd become one with the field and our friends over the summer. That's why we started pickin'. All our pay went into new gloves, but all our time together, drenched in early morning sunshine as the happier version of Children of the Corn, settled into our memory banks. I revisit that holler, the gloves, and the earwigs every time I enter a farmer's field.

Farmer Fred is the only farmer that ever hollered at me in a field. As a reporter, I'm sure many farmers want to holler at me, but I'm not their hired hand like I was Farmer Fred's. I'm the meddling hand that's getting all up in their business. But I know that if my approach is right, they'll talk.

Let them busy their hands, and they'll talk. Farmers touch their crop or the dirt their crop grows in every time they're in their field. Let them. They'll tell you their truths with seed and soil on their hands.

Joe and I stand at the intersection dividing two of his many wheat fields. His buzz cut is well groomed, his button-up ironed. His dog, a border collie named Tippy hovers at his heels. Our two trucks hog the shoulder, so we jockey for interview space without being in each other's space. He's already touched his crop, and I've already turned on my camera. We're both in our element, with dirt on our boots. Now we talk.

He tells me margins are tight, and barges make a tight budget manageable. He tells me moving grain by truck isn't feasible, more track space is unthinkable, and more fish are unlikely. He knows salmon numbers are down, but he's not convinced giving up dams will bring salmon back. The port manager agrees.

"The zeal to get something done is 'Well, let's just take these dams out and that's going to be a silver bullet, and everything is going to be okay,' but that's not the case," says David Doeringsfeld, Port of Lewiston general manager. "If just one of them is removed, that would end transportation this far inland to the Port of Lewiston."

There's a barge taking on grain by spout at the location of David's interview. He tells me 98 percent of the area's number one commodity, soft white wheat, leaves Lewiston by barge. Filling one barge takes several hours, so it's still filling when I leave David and Lewiston. I won't see river again until I reach Riggins two hours away. It's weird to be so far from the route after living it, breathing it, shooting it for so many days in a row. I have no choice but to leave it because there's no getting to it through the mountains between Lewiston and Riggins.

It's wilderness. The fish migrate out of driving range through here. I'm better off going by truck and meeting up with them in Riggins, where river meets road again.

# STEPS

CLOUDS SPILL OVER the west-facing ridge at sunset, angel dust floating down to lift our defeated and diseased spirits. I want that shot before the angels retreat. I stop setting up camp and climb into my camper for my camera. I want to show people hope as it drifts down the mountains, taking the ugly away as it glides. Even pandemics can't kill scenes this stunning.

I exit the camper backward, my camera in my right hand, tripod in my left. I shouldn't exit a camper backward with my hands full. The reasons why are painfully obvious, dangerous, and damaging. The bottom of my foot misses the step, but the back of my leg snags it, wedging my right half between the top and bottom step. My tripod hits dirt as I let go of it to slide myself free of the wedge and join it. I don't drop my already busted camera, but I loosen my grip to set it aside and start tossing around in the company of agony instead of angels. My right leg is severely beat, by a slip this time instead of a break. I don't want to put weight on it just as I didn't want to a year ago for that first step with Rod.

"Put your foot down." My therapist had said.

Nothing.

"Did you hear me?" my therapist had said again.

"Yes," I'd said looking straight ahead instead of to the left, where my therapist stood.

"Put your foot down," he commanded again.

"No,"

I'm rolling in sifted dust and prickly burrs as the foot exchange from last year continues in my mind. I see myself standing like a flamingo in physical therapy, my therapist with his plaid sleeves rolled elbow-high, holding crutches two feet out of reach.

Right before this standoff, I had had to butt-scoot across a tile floor and flop myself into a therapy pool for my workout. It's a humiliating way to have to enter a pool or any place. I had to be in warm water for weightless exercise with my rebuilt right leg, so my face was red from the heat, the workout and the scoot.

I was tired of being hurt, so I was extremely conservative on crutches. I'd leave them by the wet room entry, drop my lower half to the floor, and butt-scoot across the tile to the therapy pool. And I never wanted to talk once I slid into the pool. I wasn't being rude—I was barely holding on to my integrity and my sanity.

Lying on my side, staring at my tripod, which also lies on its side, I wiggle my toes. They move. That's a relief. I may escape this dumb decision with no more than bruises. There's no one out here and no cell service, so help isn't coming anyway. I have to self-assess. That's why I start with my toes. I know a toe routine from therapy sessions in that pool.

That workout included letters. I prefer letters to numbers, so much so that I've had my own alphabet since I was eight, and I'm constantly sorting strings of words in my mind, ever-searching for the best arrangement. If you say one sentence to me, I'll rework it in my head for two minutes and come up with at least five variations. I didn't tell my therapist about my alphabet because he already had me doing everyone else's ABCs three times. Do you know how hard it is to write the alphabet with a floating foot, especially one attached to an injured leg? Now triple your best guess on the hard scale. My assignment was one rep each set: lower case, upper case, and—when I was close to graduating from the pool—cursive.

After the alphabet, it was a butt scoot to dry clothes then crutches on carpet. I felt more respectable fully clothed, but what my therapist was asking—to put my foot down—was stupid. To make matters worse, the jerk took my crutches. I swore in that session, like I did in the session when he pushed on the arch of my deflated foot, shooting stabs of pain to my brain, which produced a lot of screaming on my part. I nearly kicked him in the face to get out of his grip. He never touched my arch again.

When that puck hit my shin, it broke two bones in three places. The Pee Wees, my younger son's hockey team of twelve-year-olds, saw coach Kris lose her cool in an extreme way when that happened. The crumple that followed impact twisted my ankle and folded the arch of my foot inside my skate. The ankle and arch injuries needed some weight to heal. My bones needed no weight to grow so sprained ankle and arch went untreated to give bone repair priority. Three months later, it was time to learn to walk.

"Stay with me here. Try. Put your foot down," he'd said, knowing I was mentally checking out while physically resisting his request.

"Give me my crutches," I replied.

"No." He leaned the crutches on a treadmill and crossed his arms. "That rod is solid. It will hold," he continued. "Put your foot down."

"How about I push you down instead?" I asked, no trace of humor in my tone.

"No. Put your foot down."

I visualized pushing my therapist down, which caused me to laugh, making me wobble. My right foot caught me before my face hit the carpet. The sole of my foot hadn't felt ground since Christmas freeze. First touch had happened at spring thaw.

I've been walking steadily with Rod since that first step out of flamingo stance a year ago, but stairs still trip me. Forward motion is tough, and backward is terrible—a bad idea for anyone really, but on day thirteen of consecutive fifteen-hour-days, I've culled a lot of bad ideas. I'd wanted that ethereal shot of heaven sliding over hills so bad that I didn't make a good decision. If Rod had an opinion, he'd call me an idiot right now while I'm rolling in dirt, while making sure I don't roll into the river.

Poor Rod. He has to share every experience with me. He's indestructible, unlike me. He won't even disappear when I die. Titanium doesn't burn during cremation. My husband will receive an urn and a rod. I told him he can use Rod to stir my ashes as he sprinkles my remains in my favorite deepest, wildest places, places most people don't dare venture but I love to haunt.

Rod's the only part of my bottom half not sporting bruises that look like mushy bananas smeared in moldy grape jelly. Like my therapist said, "Rod's solid." He'll hold, even as I'm barely holding on.

A tear drips across the bridge of my nose and puffs in the dust. I've completely maxed my want for alone time and my desire to pull off the impossible during impossible times. I miss home. I miss hugs. I miss my boys, all three of them. My husband, Hotness with a beard, and my two sons, with no beards yet but a bit of fuzz on their upper lips. We've had so much non-stop together time for the last three months during stay-at-home isolation orders that when Oregon gave me go ahead, I couldn't go ahead any faster.

There's quality time, and there's quantity time. The first few weeks of quarantine were quality. After that, quantity. We were in the same house, but not always wanting to be in the same room. I'm sure your household has had the same problem. But now that I'm away, I could really use some together time. I'm done being alone.

I have one more day of shooting on this two-week streak. I've crossed two states and two rivers off my list, with one state and two more rivers to go. I'm ahead of the fish, so I've earned some time off, starting the day after tomorrow. I'm going home dirty and bruised but not broken. I need a bath and a hug. For my family's sake, I'll bathe first.

# PART III:

## Salmon River

# FINS

BOTH SIDES OF my body are beat up, so when I wake up, I sit straight up, bumping my forehead on the ceiling of the camper. I'm back-sleeping to avoid a sore on my left ear. I won't sleep if I try lying on that side because it hurts too much. I could back-sleep or right-side-sleep before I fell out of the camper, but now only my back will suffice. My right side is bruised from hip bone to knee cap. The stairs clearly won. Rod is injury free and laughing at me.

I roll out of my bunk, brush my teeth but not my hair, and pack my lunch. Today it's salami and provolone on a crusty roll. That'll get me through the one interview I have today, then I'll restock before driving eight hours from Riggins to my home in Idaho Falls.

I'm meeting Ralph Steiner at Rapid River Fish Hatchery near Riggins, at Idaho mile 602 of 850. He has a skin-close white-and-black peppered beard, glasses, state agency-issued green fleece, and he's about to retire. I like interviewing people in the sunset of their career. They're wise and they're honest, so they know a lot and they say a lot. They tell you the truth because they're no longer worried about losing their job.

Hatcheries have some hard truths. It's hard to say salmon numbers are tanking when the counts at the dams are in the several thousands. Truth is, those thousands aren't wild born. They're manufactured. Hatcheries provide harvest opportunity. Hatcheries also inflate counts. Fish raised by the hands of humans don't feed the wild.

Rapid River Fish Hatchery is well known among fish folks. It's well respected and successful. It's owned by Idaho Power Company and operated by Idaho Department of Fish and Game. It was built in 1964 to offset the loss of salmon and steelhead due to a three-dam system known as the Hells Canyon Dam Complex. It's on the Snake River near Riggins, but it's not part of the chain of eight dams Yankee Fork fish have to cross. They divert from the Snake River to the Salmon River before the complex, but other fish runs were lost with the dams in Hells Canyon. The hatchery supplements what's lost.

The hatchery is closed to visitors during the pandemic, but the fish farm keeps churning. And it operates just as a farm does: the operators raise fish just like they'd raise chickens. The fish are fed pellet food in pens just like chickens. They're food for us, just like chickens. Unlike chickens, they may be sent to the ocean to grow up, but they're not wild fish. They're hatchery fish raised by Ralph Steiner and his farm hands, other biologists charged with replacing lost salmon runs by stocking Idaho's rivers with hatchery stock so there can be a fishing season. It's artificial. It's essential.

"There would be no fishing for steelhead and salmon in Idaho without fish hatcheries," Ralph says. "Our fish are 100 percent for fisherman."

Fish are tagged at hatcheries so they can be tracked on their journey. They're marked as manmade in a small trailer next to the rectangle-shaped raceways they're raised in. A clear tube, the diameter of the vent on a dryer, snakes from the holding tanks to the tagging trailer. The tube sucks fish into the trailer, where they're poked with a unique numbered pellet smaller than a piercing stud. Then they're sent via tube to another tank to grow before they go.

I'm not allowed in the trailer during the pandemic, as there isn't enough breathing room for an extra body, but I can go underwater in the raceways. I'm excited about this. The raceways hold millions of baby salmon. They're dense and busy, a dancing mob of lens candy.

I sanitize my underwater camera before lowering it into a raceway. The fish in there are the length of your bird finger. In this case, sanitizing isn't a pandemic precaution. It's an invasive issue. I drop my underwater camera in water all over the West. To prevent what's all over the West from invading these new fish and making them sick before they serve their purpose, sanitation is vital. It's always a good idea to clean gear one carries and wears, moving from one watershed to another. At a hatchery, it's mandatory. It costs millions to raise 3.2 million salmon. Introducing an invader wastes money.

Rapid River fish are born in Riggins, but they don't stay in Riggins. They swim to the ocean with other salmon, wild and domestic. They return as adults as planned, but not all of them make it back, which is also planned. Rapid River fish are for fishers. When you buy "ocean caught" salmon on sale in the seafood aisle at a grocery store in the Pacific Northwest, chances are high that you're buying a Rapid River fish, and you're eating hatchery salmon for dinner. It's ocean caught but not wild born. That's why it can be sold commercially.

"Twenty to forty percent of the fish that are caught in the Columbia are Rapid River fish," Ralph says. "Half the fish caught in Idaho are Rapid River fish."

Adults come back to the hatchery sometimes on their own and sometimes with our help. They arrive by the truckload to be spawned, ensuring another batch of hatchery fish for another harvest. We've used trucks to move fish forever, it seems. Before trucks, we moved train cars full of trout across the country. That's why brook trout of the East live in Yellowstone in the West. And that's why rainbow trout are everywhere. Rainbows traveled in every direction when fish stocking started. They still move pond to pond with our help by truck, plane, and packs. Browns do too. Brown trout may eat other trout, but they don't mate with them like rainbows do.

Rainbows are crossbreeding cutthroat trout out of their home waters. Like salmon, the historic range of Yellowstone cutthroat trout is shrinking. It's contentious in Idaho because the rainbows Idaho Department of Fish and Game put in by the truckload a generation ago must come out by the truckload now. Native fish that were here before us are starting to get priority over fish moved in by us. Sometimes I help with that move. It's called shocking day.

Shocking day consists of one department staffer wearing a powered pack, with a handful of volunteers following in his wake with nets. In narrow tributaries on the South Fork of the Snake Riverk, like Palisades Creek, spanning bank to bank can accommodate five people. The staffer with the pack probes the water ahead with electricity. Netters scoop stunned trout that float belly-up behind the electricity. I'm always walking the farthest behind on purpose. My right leg is titanium, and it will turn into a lightning rod if I'm too close to the juice. Being shocked on shocking day doesn't feel at all pleasant. If a little surge zings me like that, I can only imagine what a hot power line can do.

We move against the current on shocking day, experiencing the strength of spring run-off washing against us just like salmon experience it when they migrate from the ocean to Idaho. It's like a firehose in full throttle, an exhausting wash. Everyone falls more than once and up to their neck, bruising knees, elbows, foreheads. River leaks into waders that reach to your armpits. It's cold, painful, yet prudent conservation work. It's an effort to save native fish, nets full of cutthroat and rainbow trout. Only the cutties get to stay. The rainbows go.

It's not an easy decision for anyone on the South Fork of the Snake River, where the state agency started stocking rainbows in 1970. This is the era of catch and release, when fly anglers want to put hooked rainbows back in the river instead of bonking them on the head for a bounty of up to one thousand dollars. It's similar to the walleye-salmon saga, where there's a bounty on walleye in the West too.

Ralph's fish don't come with a bounty, but they're bountiful. He talks of giving back to fishers as an important part of his heritage. Just like Joe with his grain and Katie with her grapes, people providing nourishment for other people are proud of what they produce. Their crop may not help the wild, but it certainly helps us, the domestics.

# SCABS

"YOU HAVE SKIN CANCER."

There are a bunch of other words, a pause, a question, but I barely hear them.

"Are you there?"

I nod my head, realizing that the caller can't see my nod, and I must verbalize an answer.

"Yes."

"Do you want me to start over?"

"Yes."

She starts over. It's scripted. She issues the diagnosis as if she's telling me my pizza is ready for pickup. She's not a nurse or the doctor. She's the receptionist. She puts her hand over the receiver to tell the patient standing at the counter, "I'll be with you in a minute," before she continues reading the script attached to my chart. I hear her, but I don't see her. I see myself.

Myself at age seven, in that red one-piece swimsuit with white polka dots. I'm diving in the deep end of my auntie's swimming pool, hitting my head on the bottom of the pool and coming up for life-saving air with blood in my mouth and four holes in my tongue from crashing into my teeth. My mom is on the side of the pool having a fit because she doesn't know how to swim. Guess I really didn't know how either, but I do know now, and I don't dive anymore. I had scabs from that day and not just on my scalp where it scraped cement and ripped out hair. I had scabs on my nose, a sunburn so severe my nose peeled until it bled.

I see myself again, age ten, peeling skin from my shoulders, my brother's back, my sister's legs. There's so much fair skin gone red in my childhood home that I'm convinced I've found my career early in life, and it doesn't require higher education. I'm going to be a sunburn peeler when I grow up. People will pay me to peel dead skin off their bodies. I'll be so busy, I'll hire a sous-skin peeler. Like a sous-chef but for flesh instead of food.

I wasn't into tanning beds, but I liked to burn, so I'd be brown right after the skin died and right before it flaked off. My family nickname was brown bear. I have a bit more Italian in my blood than my siblings do, so I'm darker than my brother and my sister, thus the brown bear term of endearment, but I'm still fair by sunburn standards—fair enough to peel until I bleed and think I can peel others for a living.

I see myself once more, age thirteen, this time in a black-and-white striped two piece that belongs to my sister. I want to be her because she's high-school cool and I'm junior-high awkward. She has smokin' clothes and smokin' hot boyfriends. Her boyfriends are too old for me, so I steal her swimsuit instead. I wear it on my date with the sun. Its heat simmers my skin to a dangerous level because I do the unbelievable.

In that teeny tiny, zebra-patterned string bikini, I lie out in my backyard without sunscreen. No one had sunscreen in the 1980s. Tanning lotion but not sunscreen, and if the bottle accidentally had protection in it, it was only SPF 4.

As if that exposure wasn't enough, I turn up the heat by trading tanning lotion for cooking oil. Yes, cooking oil. The kind for frying nuggets, scones, and fries. The kind my mom keeps in the kitchen cupboard above the stove. That cupboard is so high, you need the pee stool to reach what's in there. Why is anything in that cupboard clear up there, anyway? Oil should be more accessible, like in the cupboard under the counter where the stockpot is.

There's canola and olive today, but back then it was only vegetable oil, gold in color and slick in application. I made sure I was out of the house and on the grass before I slathered it on my feet because I couldn't walk without slipping into a fall with it on, and back then, I already knew I didn't favor butt-scoots in swimsuits.

In case my skin soaked up cooking oil faster than the sun could sink in, I'd keep the greasy jug lid-tight and upright on the grass next to me. I didn't want any oil wasted on the grass in a spill. I needed it for reapplication. Yes, oil. I covered myself in cooking oil, and there's more to my bad burn choices. I put my oil-slicked self on a towel made of tin foil. Me, a piece of white chicken baking in the sun's oven while basting my body in oil on foil.

"Surgery is scheduled for . . ."

Oil, foil, bake, burn, bleed.

"Does that work for you?" the receptionist is asking. "Hello? Are you still there?"

I need her to start over again because I've clocked out every time she said "skin cancer" and she's said it a lot, but there's not another start. She's already asking me if I have any questions. I have a lot of questions, but none that she can answer. She's the receptionist. Receptionists shouldn't be the short straw calling with such bad news. Their bedside manner is often too abrupt. It's for calls—not cancer. I don't like it, but I get it. It's office efficiency. Someone dies of melanoma every hour. I saw it on the poster in my doctor's office. He's busy burning, freezing, and cutting cancer. He doesn't have time for calls or repeating himself three times during those calls when patients are in shock on the other end of the line.

Yes, I'm still here. You must have called the wrong number. *Click.*

# HOUSEBOATS

THERE'S NO BLOOD, no pain, no warning. Just a tooth, roots included, floating between my feet—creepy enough on its own, but it's made worse by what I'm doing when it washes up: brushing my teeth. I was studying a steep mountain on the other side of the Salmon River when something touched my toe, so I looked down. The source is hard to identify in pre-dawn light, so I wedge my purple toothbrush inside my cheek, back by my molars, and bend down for a closer look. It is indeed a tooth.

I lose my mind, my mouth frothing, thinking it's mine. I must be brushing too hard, and I'm in serious trouble because dentists don't practice in the wilderness. If this is mine, it's a permanent loss. Then I find rational. My mouth doesn't hurt, and blood isn't dripping out of it. The tooth isn't mine.

On a bluff above camp sits a historic homestead. The homesteader is buried up there. Is it his tooth? Ew. The ditches are his. As are the fruit trees once hydrated by ditches he built to divert water for his orchard. With the Salmon River declared

Wild and Scenic in 1968 and the Frank Church River of No Return corridor designated wilderness in 1980, those ditches aren't used anymore, but damage doesn't erase. Settlers blocked salmon runs on streams long before urban sprawl built walls in the river.

Surprisingly, the homesteader's apples somehow still grow in his orchard, much to the delight of black bears. Planted trees seed long after their planters pass. But I realize that the tooth isn't the homesteader's. It doesn't look human. It's shaped more for a grass chewer. Maybe a dead deer is decaying upstream, and its teeth have torn away at the roots, floating downstream toward my feet.

It's a curious find with curious timing, but since it's not my tooth, I decide it's a good omen. I finish brushing, spit paste on the beach, spit water on the paste to diffuse it, wipe foam from my face, and start filming. I want a shot of the full moon setting as the sun rises. The blue marble with pock marks slowly bounces along the points of the ridge on the other side of the river, never making a sound but illuminating, nonetheless.

After dinner yesterday, I watched the sky's night-light shine for a while in a lawn chair sunk in sand, then for more hours through the mesh top of my tent. I don't sleep directly under the stars. I'm not interested in waking up to snakes on my shins or spiders in my nose, so I sleep in a tent I can see through, rainfly optional.

I finish my sequence of moon shots before the rest of camp is lucid. I operate caffeine free, so I can accomplish a lot before everyone else has coffee in their veins. I say everyone else because I'm not alone on this stretch of the migration route. Eighty miles of the 850-mile migration route is all river, no road. It's wilderness, undeveloped. You see this section by raft and only if you win the rafting lottery. Because the pandemic has the upper hand this year, many out-of-state permit holders who won the lottery had to give up their lot. That's how I ended up part of a party with a permit. Never have I been so grateful for living in the West, where we still have vast wild within close range. We've been able to play outside within driving distance and without crowds throughout the social distance ordeal.

My family is floating with three other Idaho families in our home state. We may never draw our own permit for the Main Salmon River in our lifetime, but we ended up with a permit during the pandemic. We are four families, hockey friends, each with our house on a raft for a week. Rubber houseboats with inflatable kayaks in tow for the kids. We are roamers, traveling ten to fifteen miles a day by water and building temporary homes on a different gravel bar every night.

The first time we rafted the Salmon, we lived on the Middle Fork instead of the Main. Both require winning the permit lottery, but traffic is different on each. Horses, hikers, and rafters use both, but the Middle also had remote airstrips grandfathered in with its wilderness designation, so planes fly overhead daily. The Main's designation came with jetboats. Given a choice, I choose air traffic over river traffic. Planes are above you. Jetboats are right in front of you. Oars don't function as brakes when you need to maneuver out of a jetboat's way. It's nerve-racking, especially on S turns where sight is limited and much can go wrong without a jetboat in the intersection too.

When my heavy houseboat is an oar- and arm-powered raft, and I'm rowing toward a rapid at the same time a jetboat is motoring into it, I'm going to squirm. Jetboats, with their engines and heft, have right of way in rapids, and there are several rapids to survive every day. It's like quickly approaching an intersection at rush hour when you have the red light and bad brakes: you can see and hear oncoming traffic, but there's no slowing down.

The first raft in a party has a lookout. The lookout yells, "Boat!" like yelling, "Car!" when playing kick the can in the street. Visitors follow the same protocol on the river. It's game off for rafts when a jetboat approaches. All the rowers move their rafts to the side of the channel. I'm not quick with that maneuver, so the chaos puts me into the kind of cussing fit my husband likes to tease me about. Boulders in the flats between rapids are challenging enough. I leave the rapids to stronger rowers, like my husband. He's more sensible in rapids and around jetboats.

That said, if you're ever invited to float the Middle Fork of the Salmon River or the Main Salmon River, accept. Every time, even if you don't know how to row. A well-organized group has first-timers, one-timers, and repeat rowers. The best trips have a variety of experience. More important than knowing how to pull on the oars is knowing how to pull your fair share in camp. You don't want to help cook dinner? You won't be invited again. Everyone, including the youngest kids, has camp chores. They're worth the work in exchange for the privilege of experiencing a place that we, as a nation, have decided is worth protecting in its current form, without further development or more dollars—a place that will change your own place in this world and how you see our planet.

On my youngest son's first float trip, he couldn't sleep. He woke me up to tell me, "Someone forgot to turn off the water." That's the white noise of whitewater. It follows visitors throughout, seeping into talks and tents. There's no one out here with the power to turn off, or turn down, this water. That's why it has so much influence on our most inner thoughts, beliefs, and desires. Experiencing the liberty that comes with wild water is the best kind of undoing.

Without power, phones, or screens, the disconnect from society feels complete. That's when I focus best on the basics, on survival. And the best part of my survival is my family—my three boys. One married to me, the other two born of we.

Both sons are navigating the punches of puberty during a pandemic. They miss parties, sports, and eating out. It's late July. This is the first time they've seen their friends since early March. They haven't hung out with people their own age for four months. It's a short amount of time in the big picture, but the void—the way the pandemic is changing all of us—will shape their lives long term.

On the river, I watch my kids find some semblance of the play they lost when the pandemic started, especially my youngest. He arrived a bit more than a decade ago. Dark brown hair with curious eyes to match. He skipped crawling for wading and chooses riverbanks over bikes. He pesters his brother, questions his parents, and runs with abandon as nature intended. He's my Young Man River.

Afternoon sun catches a track of glinting medal in his mouth—his braces, for once he's not fiddling with them. In an orange inflatable kayak, wearing a yellow helmet, he's alternating arms for paddle dips. The river spreads wide and flat between rapids, safe for him to play captain.

He wears an orange Gatorade mustache, green Ninja Turtle sunglasses and no shirt under his lifejacket. He's weather kissed from his healthy shoulders to his sandaled feet in the bow of his own boat. A bald eagle lifts from a ponderosa pine on the left. A bighorn sheep steps onto the rock ledge on the right.

Captain is playing tour guide as he paddles. We're following close in our raft so we can hear his narration.

Too bad pandas don't live in Idaho. His year-end school report on black and white bears would provide an interesting list of know-it-all banter for his summer-vacation vessel. If only the banks grew bamboo.

He tucks the paddle under his legs and chugs juice like it's Dad's beer. Next, he grabs a handful of sunflower seeds, pouches them in his cheek, hands me the bag, and returns to double-fisting the paddle. He manages small steering corrections as if he were born on a boat, but backstrokes take everything he has.

When the river turns relentless in its braided, rolling pattern, he climbs out of the kayak and into the raft. Its someone else's turn to paddle because he's ready for a nap. Dad's on the oars and Mom's fishing out the front. Big brother's digging in the cooler for yet another something to snack on. Young Man River, living in a floatable, forest-green life jacket for a week, climbs onto the pile of strapped-down stuff, everything that's sustaining us for a week in waterproof, roll-top bags. He wears his hat low, sunglasses snug, and dirty toes dangling. The weave of the water rocks him to sleep like the baby he is despite his manly display of miles rowed. Despite the unease that comes with puberty and pandemics.

His nap is short, as there's a rapid ahead that won't settle for sleepers. Raft life is intense. Trees dictate home sites, so it's best to set up by them for shade, but stay away from them in storms. Bathroom habits are talked about way too much. Pee in the river. Poop in the groover, the bucket set out of sight. If you screw that up, you're on groover duty. Packing the port-o-potty is the worst kind of duty on all rafting trips, so don't confuse the order on the bathroom rule.

Raft play is intense too. Injuries are always a possibility in such a rugged place, so play with reckless restraint. In other words, go for it, but remember there's no ER if something goes wrong. We had one rapid go wrong on day two, and my chest and armpits still feel stretched beyond ordinary bounds on day four. My lifejacket doesn't fit right either. I don't have a mirror, so who knows what I look like, but something happened when the river yanked me out of the raft. I'll need further inspection when I get home.

I worry little about that because all my parts are working, and I still have my teeth. I still have cancer too. The cancer has to go, but I needed to raft the Salmon River before it goes. Stitches must stay dry, and I don't stay dry on whitewater rafting trips. Surgery is a week away, but the reason for the cuts about to come, cancer, is with me every day.

It's with me when I watch the moon set. It's with me when I row. It's with me when I hike to the homestead, throw flies at wild trout, and stake my tent in soft soil. It doesn't sneak away when I sleep, and it's there when I wake every morning. I relish those few blissful seconds of arms outstretched in cold air, with the rest of my body in the warm sleeping bag, unaware of my cancer in my sleepy haze. But then it's there, bugging me, dictating my every day.

I paint myself with white sunscreen before I dress in a quick-dry, long-sleeve hoodie. I wear a straw hat on top of the hoodie. My straw hat needs replacing, but in the nation's newfound affection for all things outdoors because pandemics force us toward fresh air, straw hats are on back order until January. I may end up duct-taping my straw hat to match my broken camera. I add multiple sunscreen applications to my daily routine too. SPF 50 in the same cinch sack as my toothbrush, lip balm and contact solution.

Prevention seems ludicrous at this point. I have cancer. Covering up doesn't make it go away but flaunting it will make it worse. It would feel like I'm proud of the problem, when I'm not. As if I want more of it, when I don't. No one wants to watch a skin cancer patient soak up more sun, then later watch her sit around the campfire applying aloe to burned skin that's already cooked with cancer.

# EARS

THERE ARE THREE types of skin cancer. Pre-cancer, kinda cancer, and serious cancer. Melanoma is serious. Mine is only kinda. I have basal cell carcinoma. Squamous cell carcinoma is the other kind of kinda cancer. I don't need chemotherapy, but I have a doctor on my cancer early. If he cuts it out, I could be cancer free for a week, a month, years yet to be seen.

The cutting isn't done in one chunk but in layers like a loaf of bread. Cut a slice, study it, cut another slice. A doctor could be a half-loaf deep before the slices read cancer-free under a microscope. The procedure is called Mohs, named after Frederic Mohs, who invented it in the 1930s. While I'm Mohs'd, my older son waits outside the building in my truck. Given the pandemic, no one is allowed to wait inside. Drivers of Mohs patients wait outside. My driver is learning to drive and to sit in the truck and wait. He volunteered to be my driver on surgery day, so he could drive my truck. He's wise in ways unrelated to steering wheels—of this, I'm sure, even as I grab the dash and stomp the floorboards because his turns are too far from the curb, and he breaks too close to the bumper ahead.

He's saving for his first car like he saved his allowance for years for his first cell phone. I split the cost with him, but at twenty dollars for monthly chores, it was a multi-year effort for that first mobile device. We picked it up on a Saturday—at least, we tried to. The sales clerk at the phone store promised a transfer from another store by ten a.m., then forgot to follow through. By our third trip in at three in the afternoon with no phone delivered, I lost my temper. Unleashing a verbal "shit" plus exclamation mark, I walked out of the store phoneless. My son followed me out with his head down like I used to do when I was little, especially if I was embarrassed.

We both knew the staff was wasting our time. We both also knew my response was a waste of everyone's time. I apologized as soon as we closed the doors on my truck.

"I'm sorry," I said, making sure my once shy eyes met his eyes trying to hide with his head angled down, chin to chest. "I'm sorry if I embarrassed you. Did I embarrass you?"

He looked up before he said anything. He busied his hands with the strings on his pale blue hoodie while staring through the windshield at nothing, everything. Then he tossed his head to the right, reframing his long blonde-brown bangs around his darker eyebrows. He made eye contact with me, those eyes that have matched his hoodie since he was born, and I knew a painful truth was coming in one sentence.

"The more important question is, did you embarrass yourself?"

I most certainly did, and I most certainly wanted to kick him out of my truck for pointing that out, but I let him stay. Wide turns and short stops aside, he's who I want waiting outside during a pandemic while I'm inside losing an ear and hoping not to gain the virus that's going around so fast that the last place anyone wants to be is in a doctor's office. Five hours into the wait, my son is about to embarrass himself. He's hungry and wishing he'd stayed home, but he doesn't want to be rude to his mom, so he keeps waiting. It takes two rounds of cut-and-study to declare my ear clear of cancerous cells. By then, I'm hungry, too, but I always hear my son in my head when I run short on patience, and I make sure I'm not about to embarrass myself. Doc is helping me fix the mess I made on my own skin. Let him take as long as he needs. I tell myself not to embarrass myself by being rude because I'm hungry, and I've been under a knife for five hours unmasked, unprotected from the pandemic.

I like my skin cancer doctor now that I'm over the shock of needing to have such a doctor in my life. He's great about letting me lie toward the window so I can see the outside world while he works. He also makes an effort to tell me what he's about to do in a way that simplifies the complicated, like what I'm trying to do with the salmon issue in this book: make hard stuff make sense.

I have small ears. I'm also younger than most of his other patients who are often retired farmers with their face, hands, and arms fried by field sun.

"The good news is that you're young, so you don't have a lot of wrinkles," he tells me through his face mask, with gloves on both hands and scalpel in his right fingers. "The bad news is, you're young, so you don't have a lot of wrinkles. That means I can't pull saggy skin from behind your ear up and over to the front to rebuild the appendage. I'm going to have to take a flap from your face."

My face. My on-camera, money-maker face. When I coached hockey, I always wore a cage over my face. Other coaches didn't. The joke in the locker room was, "Don't hit Millgate in the money maker. She needs all her teeth for TV."

It's not about vanity. It's about distraction. Reduce distraction, increase audience connection. Missing teeth are a distraction when I have something important to tell you. All this time, I've protected my face, only to lose some of it to the ears I ignored.

There's no ignoring them now. I'm numb, but I'm not deaf. Ear surgery is sound overmodulated. Scissors cutting skin sound like the exaggerated click of a potato chip bag clip. Stitches sliding through skin sound like shovels dragging heavily on cement. Stitches pulling tight for knots sound like aggressively plucked guitar strings.

When the sound affects silence, Doc hands me a square mirror with a rose-colored handle. He's not showing me the flap but the tape. Not red tape like what's holding my camera together. This tape is light brown and one inch wide instead of six inches wide. It takes a lot of one-inch strips to cocoon something, so he wants to teach me how to re-wrap what I'm leaving with. I'll be changing dressings every day.

My last hope for a less-than-obvious malformation shatters when I look in the mirror to see that I have an oversized elf ear. That's what the twenty-two dozen strips of brown tape look like herding together like sheep around my ear. There's too many sheep, so the overflow sticks to my face where my ear ends. That's where the transplant comes from. My ear stings where a chunk of it is missing, and my face aches where a piece of it is missing. I hurt, and there's no hiding it. I'm going to have some explaining to do the next time I'm on camera.

# MOMS

A NEW EAR is a lot to adjust to, but not it's overwhelming like many women say a new baby is. Many moms say motherhood is too much for them, but for me, it wasn't enough. That isn't to say it holds less value to just be a mom. "Just" shouldn't even be in that sentence, but for me it was in the beginning. I've changed my mind since, but at first, being just a mom wasn't enough.

I think it would have been enough for my mom, had she been only a mom rather than a working mom. That didn't work for her and I see it in the strain of our relationship—I always have. She worked, but she didn't want to. She had to and she resented having to. She wanted to make dinner, keep house, and hug kids. She certainly did all those things, but work bugged her. The other things didn't. She wanted those things.

As adults, we rarely see eye-to-eye, and we both know it. She keeps score so I keep my distance. I live a life she doesn't identify with, doesn't understand. She focuses on what can't be when all I see is what can be.

She raised me, my sister, and my brother with the skills she had and to the best of her ability, but she limited her ability by resenting work, fearing change, and collecting baggage.

Our relationship was strained all the time—until she fell. She fractured her back two months into the pandemic, in the depths of the strictest lockdowns. She lives in another state, so I hadn't seen her in person since Thanksgiving 2019. She went by ambulance to a hospital that allowed no visitors to enter. My mom had to wait, alone, on a gurney in a hospital hallway while she tested negative for COVID-19 before she could be admitted. None of her children, including me, showed up. We couldn't, but I'd rather not see eye-to-eye than not see her at all.

When the nurses called asking if my mom had dementia because she was being difficult and delirious, I said, "Are you sure the EMTs picked up the right lady?" That's how little I really knew about my mom's life. That realization sits like a rotten pit in my gut. Who doesn't know their mom? The mom who does more than social distance from her own mom.

The week before she fell, she called scared because earth-quakes were repeatedly rocking Salt Lake City and she lives on the third floor of an apartment. I issued sensible advice.

"Pack an emergency overnight bag. Keep it by your bed and keep a pair of shoes right there too."

The week she was transferred from the hospital to a reha-bilitation center she said, "I'm going to die of COVID in here."

She didn't. My sister made sure of it. She went to the facil-ity and did the only thing any of us could do. She looked at our mom through a window. Our mom was wearing a brace around her middle and leaning on a walker. She hated her unkempt hair, and she wanted her lipstick. The ambulance did indeed pick up the right lady.

A few weeks, later she was discharged but couldn't be home alone in her third-story dwelling, which functioned more like a treehouse without a ladder when she was in no condition to climb stairs. Being that I was the most recent recipient of a severe injury (Rod), I volunteered to live with her for a week. I dumped all I had on my plate, putting no excuse in front of my mom's needs, packed a bag, and kissed my boys goodbye.

I broke quarantine in May and crossed state lines into Utah for a family emergency. I was nervous leaving my sanitized bubble. I was anxious about being in a big city with potentially more COVID cases than my town had people. And I didn't want to go because I was mad. She didn't come for me when I couldn't walk, and that's still hard for me to understand. My husband said, "Do what you can live with." So I found the best mom I have deep within me and mothered her. That's something I can live with.

My arrival dissolved our tug of war, as I accepted her as she is and not as I wished she was. But we still argued some. I'm brave because she's afraid, but I'm afraid because she's stubborn. She won't move from the third floor. It's what she knows. She won't move to Idaho. It's too cold. She hates being alone, but she hates losing her independence more. There's no give in the negotiation, so I tapped out and took care of her in a way I didn't know I had in me.

I lived in a mask for a week because between the two facilities she was treated in, she'd been around more people than me, so I was at risk, and I didn't want to take contagion home to my family. I also kept my distance, especially when home care specialists visited to check on her progress.

I cooked, cleaned, talked to doctors, issued pills, made her do therapy, made her sit on her porch. I distracted her with movies, some of them my own. She was amazed by what I do, but I scare her and my ambition intimidates her. I explained that I'm just trying to show her how moms can be and how some moms, including me, want to be. We're fulfilled by both kids and careers. And I want to be a mom that grows as her kids need her to grow.

Each generation has its limits, but those limits expand with who we raise. I'm raising kids who will reach well beyond what I'm trying to do in life, and I want to rise to their limits, rather stronghold them with mine.

I lived with my mom a few weeks before I left for the Oregon coast. She didn't get sick and neither did I, but I was tired. City life is loud and restless. I like sleeping in the quiet of the country, or better yet, the backcountry.

I juggled pre-production plans and my mom's medication schedule. I made meals and closed deals. I wrote when she slept. I cooked while she talked. We connected over eggs for breakfast and meatloaf for dinner. I mothered and I worked and she improved.

The day I left, we were both sad to separate, but we were healthier than we've ever known. She told me she regretted not helping me when my leg was broken, and I told her I have no regrets about helping her while she was broken. It's a choice I can live with, and we're both better for it. So is our relationship.

# MEATBALLS

I AM A better mom because I am a working mom. My kids are as comfortable with a career mom as they are with a dad who cooks dinner. That arrangement is not for everyone, but it is for us. So is eating dinner together.

We dine as a family and discuss the days' highs and lows. The evening I'm back from ear surgery, when it's my turn, I tell them the high of my day was my ear officially becoming cancer free, still swaddled but cancer free. The low was another doctor telling me my chest is unhinged. No wonder my lifejacket looked crooked on our rafting trip. A skyscraper-shaking, 7.1-magnitude earthquake rapid shifted my core. My left pec sits low by my ribs. My right pec rides high by my collarbone. Doc says the odds of this happening are about as rare as one puck breaking a leg in three places.

The impact tore chest muscle, which caused one implant to rip while the other dropped. I say this between slurping up spaghetti snaked around meatballs, which I eat with a fork and a spoon that spins noodles into a tidy bite. I finish with, "I need new implants."

Around the table, my family pauses over their plates. My youngest son puts down his fork, pushes up his black-frame glasses, and says, "Wait."

He's says that often. It bugs me. He's word wasting. Starting a sentence with "wait" is useless, so I try to point out the silliness by asking, "What are we waiting for?"

That's my reply often. It bugs him. He knows why I say it, yet he resists losing the poor grammar game by using "got".

"You got fake boobs?"

Now I wait. I can tell he's not done. He hasn't picked up his fork.

"You got a boob job, and you're not a porn star?"

I put down my fork and zip up my fleece, ensuring my "job" is not on duty. My husband spits red wine, and my older son stops mid-slurp on pasta, red sauce dotting his cheeks as embarrassment bleeds across his face and mine.

"A lot of women with implants are not porn stars," I say, trying not to break eye contact or fold my arms. "They're not even in the acting business."

My implants are nearly a decade old. They should be there for another decade, but a raft and a rapid clashed in a riot and decided to force them into early retirement. The first set was optional. The second set will be mandatory. My top half isn't level no matter how I curve my spine to compensate for what's crooked. It's distracting, it's disturbing, and it's embarrassing. My chest needs straightening; its innards need replacing.

My boys were babies when my chest changed overnight. I was a new mom who cancelled her TV reporting contract and cut her hair as short as her brother's. He called me his brother-sister for a year as I massaged my head daily in a pathetic attempt to make my hair grow out faster. Let's just say it wasn't a good look on me and leave it at that.

I was living in a house full of boys, but I didn't want to look like a boy anymore. I make meatballs bigger than what could have filled my bra, the one sold in the girls' department and sized by the first letter of the alphabet. It sat like half empty Jell-O shot cups on either side of my sternum. I felt like a woman, and damnit, I wanted to look like a woman. I wanted boobs for me—not for men—so when I was done having babies, I saved enough money to buy boobs that wouldn't leave me wanting.

My boys were so young, they don't remember and I don't remind them. The decision was important when I made it. Now it's just part of the dailies. I have contacts in my eyes, fillings in my teeth, a rod in my leg, and implants in my chest. Here's your lunch. Don't miss the school bus.

The whole point of this dinner table talk was to assure them that this procedure, and its recovery process, wouldn't be as severe as the hockey injury. I answer a flood of questions: Yes, I have to wear a grounding patch in the operating room, so I don't get zapped because there's a lightning rod in my leg. Yes, they'll stay away from my ear transplant. That belongs to the other doctor. Yes, I'll be on the couch, but not for as long and with fewer drugs. I'll be coherent. I'll remember what happens, and I'll be able to move.

Both boys are looking at me, but I'm pretty sure they aren't listening to me. Neither one blinks. They're stuck on the possibility of a porn-star mother. Sorting that out lasts through dessert, brownies with pecans and no frosting.

Explaining why I'm not a porn star wasn't where I thought this dinner discussion would go, but it did. I had no idea my kids knew of stars beyond the ones we look at with a telescope in our backyard.

# DISTRACTIONS

I'M DRIVING HIGHWAY 93. It's a sunny August morning, dry earth and clear sky. I went to bed shortly after meatballs because I had an early start. I left my Idaho Falls home before breakfast and made it to Salmon, Idaho before lunch. Last night's dinner discussion is behind me and another surgery, the chest kind, awaits me after this trip. But first, fish.

I'm north of town and in a hurry. I need a canyon shot before the sun rises any higher. The light is better before full sun hits the Salmon River in this one spot. I need all the good light I can get for the bad lines I'm about to deliver around mile 706 of 850.

I'm missing a chunk of my left ear. Skin cancer claimed the top rim of it. My face and ear are covered in tape and it's obvious. It's a distraction, especially on camera. I'm doing bi-weekly updates on social media so that everyone home during the pandemic can travel the migration route with me virtually. I have thousands of screen passengers riding along. They're going to want to know what is up with my face. I can try to dismiss it, but the audience won't. I need to address it to reduce distraction. If they're wondering about tape, they aren't listening to what I say about fish. Address the distraction, then move on.

I park at the top of the empty boat ramp and walk my gear to the water line. I've had a three-hour drive to figure out what to say, yet I'm stuck on where to start. There's no one else to blame but me. Own it and get over it.

The Salmon River is shallow where I stand. It runs over smooth rock with just enough babbling to drown traffic noise on the highway next to it. Beyond the babble, the river drops into a deep pool, silently changing from the color of whiskey to the color of gin. I prefer natural sound in the background over engine sound, so I position myself by the ripple and confess my sins like I'm about to drop into the deep pool and must spill my own tea before I do. I look at the red blinking light and spill.

"I have skin cancer," I say without visibly flinching. "I lost a chunk of my left ear because of it. That's why you see tape on the left side of my face. We're still following salmon, but this—" I pause to point to my taped left ear. "—is a distraction. Let's address it, then put it away and get back to fish."

My confession continues. I know it word for word now because I've watched this recording no less than seventy-nine times in the edit bay.

"I knew I had a problem because I had a sore on the top ridge of my ear that wouldn't heal from January through June, but due to COVID-19 restrictions, I wasn't exactly eager to be sitting in a doctor's office. The sore really festered while I was on the road through Oregon and Washington because I wore a hat every day while covering salmon migration, and hats rub on ears.

"By the time I reached Idaho, I had a confirmed diagnosis: skin cancer. I had surgery a few days before arriving here, on this stretch of the Salmon River. By the time migrating salmon make it this far, they're starting to look pretty hammered, so the irony of me also looking hammered is freaky and uncomfortable.

"My ear stings because the top part of it is missing. It was cut off along with the cancer. My face aches, too, because part of it is also missing. It was sliced off and put on the top of my ear as replacement skin. I'm good about protecting my face when I work outdoors, but all these years I forgot my ears.

"I'm not here to lecture you about covering up or wearing sunscreen, but I will tell you this. It is painfully humiliating to lose a chunk of your body because of your own actions. Skin cancer addressed. Let's move on."

I reach for the red button, stop recording, and stop thinking about cancer. Not for good, but for now. We have fish to follow.

# CRUCIFIED

I SEE BLOOD, pearls, power lines, and beams. I slow, park, stare. It's a cross. No church, just a cross. An artist's sacrificial offering to thee unholy. No blessings come with this ceremony on the side of the road. Maybe I should have done my cancer confession here instead.

Upon closer inspection, I see that the blood is red paint. It's dripping from rusty nails staked in a salmon's front gill and the base of its tail. The salmon isn't real but made of metal. The pearls, cheap party beads, dangle out of the salmon at its belly line. They represent fish eggs, spawn spilling down the post. The power lines are black chords draped over a horizontal wood beam nailed to a vertical trunk of tree milled in the shape of a power pole. It's a crucifix.

It's salmon sacrificed for power. I confess, I never thought I'd see this, not anywhere along the 850-mile trek. But if I'm going to see it, it would be in Idaho. The salmon situation seems more extreme in Idaho than it does in Oregon. Can you imagine this cross ending up on Beacon Rock in the Gorge?

That would unravel a lot of people. If Oregon starts feeling the angst Idaho feels, we're really seeing the last of salmon.

Idaho is the fringe for these fish. It's the heart of salmon migration—their crib and their grave—but it's also the far reaches. When wild animals start blinking out, the fringe is the first place to lose their presence. Idaho is losing salmon. Fishing seasons are shortened or closed altogether in the Gem State, with too few fish to be handled or hooked. The difference is apparent in the fish I don't see and the people I do see. They cry during interviews.

Crying on camera is a personal reveal deserving respect. When its sincere, it's sacred. I don't zoom in for a tighter shot on a tear. I don't prod for more emotion. I don't move when someone is moved. If a question triggers sadness during an interview, I let that person gather themselves however they can and continue. I'll stop rolling if they ask me to, but most often they don't. The truth is in their anguish, and sometimes it comes with tears.

When Lytle Denny, an anadromous fish biologist, talks about learning to spearfish salmon with his dad in the 1980s, he cries. He's a member of the Shoshone-Bannock, a Native American tribe in Idaho. His tribe is known as the Agaidika, the salmon eaters. As their primary food source disappears, so does his tribe's identity.

"It's tough to hear extinction and salmon. I don't want to be part of that," Lytle says. "That's sad that we're even getting into that realm."

We've talked about his heritage by phone. I'm interviewing him in-person at the Yankee Fork tomorrow. He's updating me via text as the fish arrive, so I know I'm on track. There aren't many, but there are some. They swam past the crucifix I'm staring at.

A flatbed farm truck appears behind my art-deco, fish-wrapped truck while I'm shooting footage of the crucified. A bearded man gets out of the driver's side and approaches. When he's within six feet of me, I stop rolling and step back. Beards terrified me when I was little: I thought hairy faces had something to hide. I know better now. Beards are no indication of character, but I still step back. I'm on the road solo, and we're in pandemic times. I'm not used to having a stranger in my personal space. Plus, I'm unmasked because I was alone. I have to unmask as much as possible to reduce irritation on my new ear.

The bearded man is unmasked, too, but he is often. He's not worried about a virus he doesn't think is real, but he's interested in my truck camper. A lot of people drive trucks in rural Idaho, so it's common conversation starter. I tell him how my rig performs in the backcountry around the valley he lives in and why it's wrapped in fins, marking me as the journalist following salmon from the ocean to Idaho.

He's aware of the angst over anadromous fish, fish born in freshwater and raised in saltwater like salmon are. It's nearly impossible to live in Salmon, Idaho and not be aware of the angst. Plus, he frequents the highway, so he's seen the crucifix before, but he hasn't seen me. That's why he stopped.

I'm approachable. I have to be if I want strangers to tell me their secrets during interviews. I also have to listen even when I don't like what strangers say, and I can tell I'm not going to like what I'm about to hear. My mouth is already slack jaw behind my mask. Another thing masks hide: discontent subliminally shaping your lips.

He's cordial enough. He knows my work, asks where I'm going, and how it's going. I'm not the boasting type, but my elevator speech lasts several floors if you really want to know what it's like to do my job most often as the lone woman in the woods with beards, sharing the wild's story with those unable to work outside for a living.

Someone once told my husband, "That's a lot to be married to." The "that" referred to me. Whenever one of us is too over the top about something, that's the ease-up line between us, and I can tell that's exactly what this guy is thinking. I'm a lot to be married to.

When his questions run out, he scratches his beard. I switch from video camera to photo camera during the scratch, hoping we're done. We're not. He takes off his ballcap with his right hand, ruffles his sandy-colored hair with the same hand, and puts the cap back on. I remove my lens cap, wondering why he hasn't gone back to his own truck to leave, since I've stopped talking. I'm working. Verbally, I nudge him away with, "Thanks for stopping. You have a nice day."

He's done being cordial, but he doesn't give me his back. He wants the last word.

"This wouldn't work for anybody else," he says, shoving his hands in the front pockets of his jeans and extending his belly like a male sage grouse. He's strutting rudely. "You've only made it this far because you're pretty."

He puts extra pressure on the *P*, popping it with so much force, spit sprays from his lips. I step back again. No one should be sharing spit during a pandemic. I'm uncomfortable, but I smile, enlisting my confusion tactic. Smiling makes the attacker think I'm okay with what he's saying so I can be sure he listens when I tell him I'm not okay with what he's saying.

Avoiding my stitches on the left, I raise my right index finger and tap the right side of my head between my hat and my brow, gesturing brains rather than beauty.

"Mister, you're mistaken," I say. "I've only made it this far because I'm pretty ambitious."

Now everyone loitering around the cross has confessed. Seeing salmon crucified brings out the bold in all of us.

# PART IV:

Yankee Fork

# BUSTED

I GRAPPLE WITH anxiety this close to the end, river four of four, mile 828 of 850. The once tortured and now transformed Yankee Fork awaits. Its mouth spills into the Salmon. I feel small in this landscape. The gravel piles bury my shadow. The dark canyons swallow my sight. But the fish. Oh, the fish. I spot Chinook salmon far longer than anything that's ever taken my line, but I'm not here to hook up. I'm just here to look with my lens, capture the images. I start with my drone.

I leave my tripod in the truck to avoid carrying it as it knocks on my shoulder bones trudging through the forest. I'll be moving around with a remote while flying my drone, which is lightweight and keeps its distance. At this point, I'll do almost anything to keep equipment far from my stitched and taped body parts for a little bit longer. I'm sure I'll hit a stitch with one camera or another later today, but not with the drone. So I start the day with that.

The Yankee Fork of the Salmon River leans on the back of the Frank Church River of No Return Wilderness. There's no cell service, so I called wildfire dispatch last night before I drove up the deep-carve canyon between Challis and Stanley, Idaho. The highway leashes the Salmon River all the way up, but other modern-day conveniences disappear as thorny brown brush turns to needle green trees with elevation rise. Regional command centers across the West monitor wildfires in forested public land like the Salmon-Challis National Forest. I've spoken with rangers of this forest often during this project, sometimes even arguing with them.

Federal orders prohibit filming in areas designated as wilderness. There are a lot of obvious reasons why this is necessary. Hollywood shouldn't be able to chop protected woods, move in talent trailers, and build a movie set on site that permanently alters the unspoiled scenery for a one-time deal. But I am not a mega-movie house. I'm a freelance journalist who knows how to tell stories through video. My footprint is no larger than a backpacker's, and I don't have crew, yet I must apply for permission to shoot footage in the forest, and I must pay for that permission, just as Hollywood does.

The charge for one day of shooting footage from a raft on the Main Salmon River is more than the total amount of money a newspaper pays me for my story. The system is busted. That's one of the reasons why I work for so many outlets at once. Media outlets don't have big budgets anymore. They don't have the backing to pay for big stories. They want them, and their audiences want them, but they can't afford them. I can't afford to work for free no matter how much I want to cover a story. Freelance isn't free because free doesn't feed my family.

Freedom of the press doesn't mean I'm free to work for free. It means I'm somewhat free of the trappings someone may try to apply when I'm trying to do my job. In short, the constitution declares it unconstitutional for anyone or any entity to prevent me from doing my job as a journalist just because they don't like the way I'm doing it or what I'm saying. The Forest Service says they're not dictating what I cover; they're just mandating that I have to pay for a permit to cover it. Requiring me to get a permit, whether staff likes my story or not, is still a First Amendment violation. It prevents me from doing my job unless I pay and possibly even if I do pay.

Just as preventing a flag burner from singeing our stars and stripes violates freedom of speech and preventing someone from praying in public violates freedom of religion, forbidding me from getting the story without paying for it is a breach of my right. And it's possible that the Forest Service could delay my permit for so long that I'd miss the story altogether. Holding the permit process over my head to keep me out of a story that makes someone look bad also violates freedom of the press.

Just as biologist Bob Wertheimer at Bonneville Dam considers salmon recovery serious, I consider freedom of the press serious. It's my privilege and my burden to report fairly and accurately despite obstacles, easy ways out, popular vote, public perception, and preconceived notions. There's no benefit to doing my job wrong. Do mistakes happen? Yes. Are they intentional? Not by me. I gain nothing by conjuring fake news into my reporting. That's an oxymoron. If it's fake, it's not news. It's just fake information. It is mortifying to see a profession I give my credibility and my career to being dragged through oblivion just because it reports what someone doesn't want to hear. There's a legitimate reason my job is protected by the Constitution of the United States. Rue the day our nation, like other nations, must rely on a supply of information that only funnels the words we want to hear.

The more confusing aspect of the First Amendment argument is the lack of pull the press actually has when push comes to shove. Sure, some media moguls knock heads with the feds over permits for stories, but I must work two hours to pay my attorney for one hour of his time and settling the permit issue in court is going to take more than one hour and more than one journalist. I'll miss deadline. I'll miss the fish, so I pay the permit and make less than the permit costs to cover the story.

Those permits, once processed, come with restrictions. They're not a free for all. My permit for filming from a raft for one day while on the Main Salmon River for one week prohibits drones. My cameras date-stamp video files so I have proof I only shot for one day, the exact permit-issued day, if ever I'm asked, but for my sake and the ranger's, I didn't take my drone on the rafting trip. That avoids raising the slightest suspicion of violating a permit that violates my professional, protected rights.

I am cleared to fly my drone over the Yankee Fork because it is not designated wilderness, but I must also be permitted to fly it by the Federal Aviation Administration (which requires money and a test every two years), and I must call fire centers for clearance before launch. If there's a fire, there's no flying. If there's a fire, all my tests, permits, and payments are for nothing, and there's no refund.

Before I lost signal, I reached out to dispatch to check off the last limitation in the way of my aerial footage. There's smoke in the air. There's smoke in the air everywhere this late in the summer, but nothing is burning in the drainage I want to fly with my drone. I'm cleared.

Smoke or not, if I'm in a plane's strike zone, that plane is in serious trouble. I'm a nervous pilot. I fly low and slow. The flight seems high and fast to me when I'm operating the remote control on the ground, but in the air, I'm too conservative for aviation acrobatics. If a real plane is flying as low as my drone, it's in trouble with a mechanical malfunction.

I want the overhead angle and I'll get it, but I won't dink around when I'm up there. Lift, record, land. Nothing else, especially over water. I pit out my shirt every time I fly over a surface that can sink my shot. The Salmon River is water you won't retrieve equipment out of, so if your propellers kiss ripples, kiss them goodbye. Rapids eat dropped drones, and you'll be left starving. That's why my pits sweat and my hands shake. I've never dumped a drone in a river, and I don't plan to today.

I'm ready to launch as soon as enough daylight slides over the pine-pocked ridge. This section of the forest hasn't burned yet, so trees are still brilliant instead of black. A light sprinkle overnight brightens the plants and dampens the dust. The soft breeze is harmless, but I'll have to keep vigilant watch for raptors. They won't like me snooping on high. I'll drop altitude immediately if feathers approach.

I'm standing where the Salmon and the Yankee Fork meet. From the fish's upstream point of view on its return trip from the ocean, the Yankee Fork is a right turn off the Salmon. There's force coming out of that fork and force coming from the main channel. The two meet, picking up speed as the race to send drops to the Pacific Ocean continues. I fly higher than I'm comfortable with right here. The turbulence of the two colliding stirs trouble I don't want to mix with. The goal is to keep the lens high and dry while recording what's wet below.

Less than half a mile upstream from the confluence, I spot an obtrusive heap of crumbling, lumpy cement. It's in the Salmon River. What? That isn't right. The Salmon is dam free. All 425 miles of it. No dams. We already talked about it being one of the last, and longest, stretches of wild water in the nation. I look closer at the clump of concrete displaying on the screen. My drone is spying on a man-made relic. It's most certainly a dam, but it's busted. It's Sunbeam, built in 1910 and blown up in 1934.

Sunbeam generated hydropower for a gold mine for one year before the power plant cost more than the minerals pulled out of the mining district with its energy. If historical accounts are accurate, Sunbeam actually blew up twice: for the first time, and officially, by a game warden, and for a second time, off the record, by fishermen who saw salmon running into it.

I fly my drone over the debris, knowing rafts shouldn't go in there. There's a lot in the way, but water passes and so do fish, unless they're Yankee Fork fish on their way home. Those salmon turn right at the fork below Sunbeam.

Next, I fly the mouth of the Yankee Fork, spotting three rafts already in pre-launch stage before breakfast. From above, they look like three oversized, white, pre-toasted campfire marshmallows on the screen I reference when checking the overhead angle of my drone shots. They must belong to day trippers starting their float on the Salmon below the old dam site so they don't have to battle what's left of it. Wise decision.

I pilot my morning mission up the Yank, taking stock of the cream-colored columns supporting the highway overpass that act as entrance. They're a modern-day welcome to a place that doesn't want to advance as fast as we do, but still, it sends its liquid life into the basin to refresh our conquests, anyway. My lens in the sky absorbs water so clean and clear, my eyes water with thirst. The ripples in the cascade are created by the kind of rocks I want to slide into my pocket for safe keeping, but I leave them in their chosen pouch in the river. They show best there. They're designed by time before traffic with a palette that spectrums from deep purple to pumpkin orange, from cinder red to dazzling gold. Some of the stones are in fact gold. That's how this place landed on my radar in the first place. Gold.

Gold diggers dredged more than one million dollars' worth seven decades ago. Mining and logging took their piece of the place too. When the resource ran dry, they moved on. It was the era of rush before bust. They didn't take their busted stuff with them, and they didn't clean up after themselves either. They left it, but some divine intervention beyond our simple programming somehow convinced a few Chinook salmon to deem the dead pools their home. Because of the Chinook, the Fork is getting a facelift.

It's decade one of a multi-year, multi-agency watershed restoration effort. I first saw the project in 2016, when I laid on a beaver dam in backcountry and hatched this grand plan to follow salmon migration from the ocean to Idaho. Cassi Wood was here then, and she's still here. She eagerly babysits the restoration process, knowing she's leaving the Yankee Fork much better than she found it.

"As soon as you see the fish come in, you know you've done something right," she says. "Fish are such an important part of our heritage, that without them, I don't really think we're complete."

I finish flying my drone over the dredge, then walk the river with Cassi, looking for what makes us complete. Three Chinook salmon, recent arrivals from the ocean, swim along the edge of the construction zone. It seems they like the look of the improved landscape already. They hide under a newly built log jam, fins waving slow like sea fans in deep ocean.

They remind me of the motion sick teenager at the bottom of the roller coaster exit ramp. He loved the beginning of the ride, but he hates the end. All the jostling, jerking, and struggling to keep his hands inside the ride and his head attached to his neck did him in. He moves slowly. He sees in spins. Once off, he rushes to hug a garbage can.

Chinook look the same at the end of their ride. Anything that was in their belly when it started has evacuated. They don't eat during migration, so whatever back fat they're carrying when they leave the salty ocean and enter the freshwater inland system must sustain them until they get off the ride. They're running on empty, but they're not hungry. They have that *what-just-happened?* look. They swim slow, spin a bit, and need to hug a log.

We let them be and walk along banks crafted so recently that they're bare of plants, but by next summer sprouts will line both sides of the Fork. Rock sprawls out everywhere. The dredge spit out penny-sized pebbles and mixing bowl-sized boulders. The loose piles, some hip-high, others their own hill that needs climbing, shift and rearrange every time they're stepped on. Visitors must place their feet with purpose here. Slips and slides are common.

Cassi is surer footed on cobble than I am with the rod in my leg, so she slows her steps to stay even with me. I let her. I don't need to fall and break another camera or rip a stitch. I don't know if she slows on purpose, but I know I slow on purpose around people advancing gingerly.

I refuse to rush past people limping toward the grocery store. Do you know how far away the entrance is from the parking lot? I do. It's miles. Miles, I tell you. The first time I went grocery shopping with Rod, I was spent before I reached the carts stacked by the glassed, sliding-door entry. We easily dismiss short distances and simple tasks when we're able, but we face a fierce reckoning when we're the person struggling to put on a shoe and walk all the way to that entrance.

I'll never forget my own reckoning the first time I went to the store with my new leg. I was mad at myself for being slow. I was frustrated with a limb built by man rather than born of my parents. I didn't like the physical change with no "undo" option, and I really hated the loneliness of coping with trauma on a level most people can't relate to. Still today, when someone says, "Be careful. You're fragile." I get angry. There's no way I'm fragile physically. I'm rebuilt with titanium. Financially and emotionally fragile, maybe so. That rebuild is in process. It's fragile with fierce on its heels, and my fierce side comes out when people say, "What's the big deal? You broke your leg. Move on."

The big deal isn't physical. Tools fixed that. Losing more than half of my business while growing bone on the couch, that won't be fixed with a rod. Neither will the reality of vulnerability or the loathsome worry I permanently carry after a life-interrupting injury. The havoc of adjusting my ambition to accommodate my health problems, whether it be broken bones or skin cancer, is like a full garbage can knocked on its side during a windstorm, lid circling in chaotic bursts. I'm trying to gather myself, collect my sanity, and put things back where they belong. Things like my memory, my motivation, my spirit. I didn't want to pick up the cards I was dealt, so the dealer shoved them in my mouth and now I'm chewing on them. I'll break them down eventually.

That's the dialogue running through my head every time I walk toward a grocery store. That's why I'll never again speed walk to get in front of a slow walker trying to go inside a grocery store for the necessity of food, when I know they feel awful.

Cassi's subtle adjustment to my new pace is evident, but not amplified. I'm able, just not as fast as when we first walked these wobbling stones in 2016. She doesn't offer me a hand, and I don't want her to. I don't need a hand. Neither does she. Cassi is small in stature, especially in her oversized waders, but her plans are grand and she's as organized as the landscape she's designing. She's Trout Unlimited's central Idaho project specialist. With dark curly hair, aqua eyes, and dimples, she's friendly in conversation but intense in her efforts.

She coordinates progress with tribes, government agencies, industry funders, non-profit organizations, and private contractors who all want the same result: more Chinook salmon swimming 850 miles from the ocean to Idaho to spawn. But the thinking was different seventy years ago, when the dredge ripped the river apart. Fixing what's busted won't wipe the slate clean. Far from it. Mining's heritage in Idaho runs as deep as the mineral's veins. That's why the dredge and the tailings left behind by dredging are protected as part of the Gem State's history.

The dredge, now a tourist attraction, stays. It's a massive, invasive reminder of the way the Wild West was tamed. Even in powered-down sedation, it has its way with the Yankee Fork. Seven miles of gravel spit out by the dredge choke the river, cut off channels, and block salmon migration, but each year, another stretch of destruction is repaired. Some of the tailings will stay, but the rest is returning to the river for salmon's sake.

# PLANTERS

CASSI WORKS THE lower end of the drainage while Lytle stages higher—so high he's beyond the rusty dredge, the abandoned mine, the ghost town, and the graves. Salmon that make it clear up here deserve to do whatever they want, wherever they want, and Lytle is hoping they will.

Lytle is my last interview on the route. He's number seventeen. I talked with hundreds of people before I narrowed down my interviews to seventeen perspectives. Cassi was the only interviewee I knew before I started migrating. I found the rest of the interviewees with help from other people who also claim salmon country as their country. Investigate an issue people are interested in, and they'll most often respond in droves.

Cassi told me about Lytle, but Lytle hesitated to talk to me the first time I called him. The Shoshone-Bannock Tribes must approve of the media interacting with its members, especially when it comes to salmon, which is Lytle's life's work as a tribal member and a fish biologist.

The Shoshone-Bannock live on Fort Hall Reservation less than an hour from my house, but I can count on one hand the number of times I've shot video with the tribe in the last twenty-plus years. Some of the blame falls on me, but some of it results from the tribe's hesitancy to speak with members from the media. They don't want the media, or white people, meddling any more than they already have.

Those handful of video shoots include one wildfire assignment. I showed up with my camera alongside a ranger with orders to evacuate the burning reservation, so I didn't get far. No one would leave, and no one would talk.

The other story was a cattle drive. One rancher had permission to move cows across the far northwest corner of the reservation. I only had permission to shoot the story from the road, which anyone could drive. I couldn't step off the black top, or I'd be trespassing on tribal land. Fortunately for me, cattle drives, like drivers, don't stray too far from the rumble strips.

I also worked with the tribe on an ad campaign. I was hired by a rodeo committee to shoot footage for a TV commercial. That video shoot came with a lot of limits, a couple of which stood out to me most. First, women were not allowed to touch the feathers on a headdress. I'm a woman so I couldn't touch no matter how out of order a feather might have strayed. And second, the tribal member riding bareback in the ad had to be paid on site. The paying agent handed cash to the rider before he dismounted. I didn't get paid for two months.

As a traditional news reporter, it's unethical for me to pay people to talk to me because payment turns credibility into bribery. As it is, I'm relieved when I'm paid by an outlet, and there's never extra money for paying people to talk to me, anyway. They either talk or they don't. Money isn't a motivator, so the message has to be, and Lytle's message is strong, both personally and professionally. He's the last of my seventeen interviewees, but I can already tell he'll be the first voice you hear in my finished film, *Ocean to Idaho*.

"I have dreams about what full salmon runs look like. I can see it. I don't know if that's normal, but it is for me," Lytle says. "It's not just about salmon recovery. It's about our connection to this earth."

He talks with sincere purpose as he works by the creek, shaded from the high-elevation sun. For my skin's sake, I should dress more like Lytle when I'm in the field, covered and nearly cancer-proof. His long-sleeved shirt is blue-sky bright. His straw hat drapes like golden honey wrapped around thick, dark brown hair.

Where he's parked, the water is considered untainted by modern day—no mess to clean up. The thin river is barely fifteen steps wide with thick willows shoring up both sides.

"In the mid 1980s, we started fixing habitat in the Yankee Fork, and we're still doing it," Lytle tells me as he opens the tailgate on his truck and pulls a large, smelly clear sack out of the bed. "We're still trying to improve fish habitat, but by and large the habitat is vacant."

The vacancy he's referring to is the void left by salmon. They're food for us and for the forest. Lytle fished the Fork growing up. Tribal elders pass spearfishing techniques from one generation to the next. Lytle remembers many fishers but few fish. The run was already running out in the 1980s, food for the masses no more.

The sack he pulls to the edge of his tailgate contains food. Raw, quickly spoiling in the sun fish flesh. Lytle carefully pulls it free of the plastic and starts walking with food. But it's not his food this time. It's the wild's. A spawned and spent Chinook running the length of his leg swings heavy in his right hand. It's a hatchery fish, so it can't be counted as made by nature. That's why its tail is missing. Eventually all of it will be missing, the decay of death sprouting new life 850 miles from the Pacific Ocean. Lytle lays the lifeless animal in the stream, steps back, and watches the dead drift toward an old aspen. Its trunk is horizontal rather than vertical, so the bark drinks instead of the roots. Deadfall. Bugs zoom in with haste when the fish hangs up in gravel shallows, flies feasting on foul meat within a minute.

What I'm seeing doesn't make sense. Why is the food floating away? Lytle explains with the kind patience, serious clarity, and aged wisdom that comes from keeping Mother Earth close in all actions. He's speaking for his tribe. When Chinook salmon returned by the thousands a century ago, their sodium-rich, ocean-grown carcasses naturally added nitrogen and other needed elements to landlocked freshwater forests. Now, only a few dozen fish make it this far. Lytle is trying to make up for the loss by putting dead hatchery fish in the river. They're purposely placed planters, there for nature, not us.

"I'll never give up trying to save these salmon," he says, with trembling in his conviction. "I'm always thinking of ways to get more fish. You gotta keep going. This is a fight. We're fighting for the salmon, and it's good to see that they're still fighting too."

Lytle sewed planters a stitch further into the food web one summer. His fisheries crew measured and tagged bull trout in July. Those trout live in tributaries that should host Chinook salmon. Salmon migrating from the ocean to Idaho spawned in August then died. Lytle and his crew recaptured the tagged bull trout in October and measured their growth, repeating the research in four similar streams, but those actions created scenarios that were far from similar. They called it their Dr. Seuss Study because of the differences in each stream: no fish, fake fish, dead fish, real fish.

The stream with bull trout and no salmon was their growth baseline. The stream with fake fish, or ground salmon pellets, showed minimal growth when compared to the baseline. The stream with dead salmon planted by the tribe showed some growth, but the stream with live salmon spawning and dying showed significant growth. No other scenario, not even dead planter fish, came close.

"There's nothing like having live fish in a stream," Lytle says. "We understand that the natural process is the best, but we are not in a situation where we have thousands of fish to rely on."

Lytle watches flies feed on the dead fish he just planted. He knows those flies feed bats and birds. He know bears and badgers may feed on the fish too. They'll also carry parts of it from the river to the woods, or spread it even farther when they go to the bathroom. Berries have been known to sprout in bear poop. There's no reason fish food can't spread the same way, as long as there are fish.

Fish have to mate to have more fish, and that's what I worry about as I watch the morbid yet nutrient rich scene play out. The only fish I see with Lytle is dead. The only fish I saw with Cassi were hiding. No one is getting lucky. The fish down low are not ready. Up high, they haven't arrived, maybe they won't ever. Records indicate my timing is spot on, but something is off. The fish decide when to spawn, not us. Their time doesn't always jive with our wishes. The day slides to dim, and I know I'm done. The August spawn isn't happening in August.

I retreat. I take off my wading boots, my waders, and my socks. I plant my bare feet in clean stream and connect, plugging into nature's grid. It's my last act since the fish aren't performing their last act. My toes tingle with chill as my grand finale floats away with the severed tail of the planter fish. I'm going home empty-handed.

# STITCHES

ANOTHER WHALE-SIZED WALL of water rolls toward the raft. My knuckles turn white as I squeeze a handle, hoping my hold is strong enough. That wall will swamp us—or worse yet, a swamping with an aggressive spin cycle. The hockey mom on my right spins first, and I grab her thigh. My armpit stretches like pulled taffy, but she stays in the boat. I spin next. I'm out, but I'm still holding on. My left armpit pops like the lid on a canning jar of pickled preserves. Because I'm still holding on, I land in the raft instead of the river. Guess my hold was strong enough. My chest burns like coffee spilled on crotch.

I come up for air, falling off the couch. I don't feel wet, but my face, head, and chest throb with pain. And why is there wood under my cheek instead of water? Open ears. No rapids rushing. Open eyes. No river rolling. I didn't lose the blue raft. I lost my claim on the black couch. That damn black couch. I'm living on it again. I'm on drugs again. I'm having nightmares again. I was only out for a year, and now I'm back in. Last go around, a grizzly in my grill had startled me out of my pain-pill snooze. This time, it's raft gone wrong in a rapid. But it really did happen. That's why I'm on drugs. I lived it. Now the muscle memory of it plagues me in my dreams.

I gather myself off the living room floor and go to the kitchen. I'm assessing damage as I shuffle. My shirt hasn't stained, but I can feel something running down my neck. I tell my husband to stop rummaging around in the kitchen and look at me. He's so absorbed in hounding the boiling pot he needs for dinner prep that he didn't hear me hit the floor. I ask him to check my ear as I remove tape and gauze. He looks. He gags. He returns to rummaging.

There's a disgusting mess of ooze and blood on the left side of my face, so his response doesn't alarm me. I'm pretty sure he would have mustered some type of warning if I'd popped a seam. As it is, his revulsion tells me the scene is still intact. I recover, wash my hands, grab an eleven-ounce bag of Goldfish from the kitchen cupboard, a thirty-ounce bag of Swedish fish from the kitchen closet, and return to the couch. I'm here to heal and to sulk, waiting for my turn on the disaster train to be over. I thought for sure it was when I learned how to walk on a limb rebuilt with titanium.

This sit-in will only last days rather than months, and for that I'm grateful. I shove three Goldfish and two Swedish fish in my mouth and chew while I stew. The couch sits at a different angle this year, so I see different walls this time. The walls in my house are hangers for the photographs I've shot while on assignment as an outdoor journalist for more than two decades. How I display my work—as art—is my way of bringing the outside in. Eagles, trout, mountains. Visitors see the outdoors when walking into my house. I've changed one wall grouping since I learned to walk. It's the one seen when entering my home through the front door.

That wall used to welcome visitors with the wildlife of Grand Teton National Park: moose, marmot, bluebird, buffalo. I swapped the visuals of one place for the look of a lot of places that have a common theme. Moving water. The kind that moves me and hopefully moves everyone else if I shoot it right. It's also the kind of water that moves fish, Chinook salmon in particular. Their birthplace and their deathbed are supposed to be the same place. What they swim through to come full circle is on my wall now: Columbia River, Snake River, Salmon River, Yankee Fork.

I'm still following migration, but I'm ahead of the fish and behind on my health. I'm falling apart. That's why I'm home. My ear and face are stitched. My chest, both pecs, are stitched too. I've accumulated new seams in four places like a scarecrow on the couch instead of on a cross. Hold still. Stay with me.

# POISON

MY NEW CHEST is settling into place. That doctor is pleased, but I plead for relief on a Sunday morning as I settle in a reclined surgical chair under the concerned stare of my other doctor, the skin cancer specialist. My next appointment with him was scheduled for three days away, but I wouldn't last that long. This is an emergency. I sat up overnight waiting for a decent hour to call him. Is there ever a decent hour for a work call on a weekend? No, but when I called him with urgency in my voice, he met me at his office, on a Sunday, in less than an hour. It's the first time I've called the in-case-of-an-emergency number given after surgery, but it's well warranted. So warranted, that I probably should have skipped waiting until sunrise and called him in the middle of the night. I'm hysterical and beside myself in a manic state of scratch.

Both docs told me no outdoor galivants right after surgery and I obeyed, but somehow I have a poison ivy problem, anyway. Or rather, poison ivy by proxy. I'm having a severe reaction to something on my head, and I want to yank at it until my hair falls out.

I lie on my right side so skin cancer doc can work on my left ear, the epicenter of the problem. I want to stab at it until it bleeds and the skin sloughs off so there's no more itch. Doc starts ripping tape away from my head. My eyes roll back in my skull. It's like taking off a tight beanie. You must put your fingernails to your scalp after that to enjoy the release with an aggressive itch. It feels like that, but multiplied by one hundred.

He pulls off glue and gauze next. My left foot kicks on my right calf like a dog receiving a long-begged-for belly rub. It's so satisfying, I ask him to reattach all the medical supplies and tug again. He doesn't do it, but I really want him to.

In the movie Hitch, the character played by Will Smith has a reaction to shellfish. His ear swells beyond double its normal size. That's me right now. My ear looks like a tuba tacked on my cheek. A beet-red tuba with ooze leaking out of it like a drip hose. Spreading from this eye of the storm is more red flesh and burning bumps creeping into my hairline, down my neck, and across my face.

My ear is revolting and I know why. It's a pathetic collection of pieces, a puzzle with shapes forced together in some semblance of wholeness, but not really. My body is supporting the revolt with a rash beyond human tolerance.

This situation birthed itself after a death. My first skin transplant didn't work. It died. Died! My face died trying to live on my ear. That was not supposed to happen. I'm fit. I don't smoke. I should be able to grow skin no problem, but I didn't. A chunk of me withered on the rind of my petite, delicately curved hearing device. Unacceptable. I don't have enough face to have part of it dying. If this is what I go through for every part I lose to skin cancer, I won't last long. The "you're healthy" card can only be played so many times before it expires.

Another chunk of my body, this one from the narrow, smooth sliver of flesh between the back of my ear and my hairline, is now living on the top of my ear. It's embalmed in gauze, glue, and tape—a layered cast, and within it, my fragile ear is sewn flat to my scalp for better blood supply. To keep it flat, Doc has added more glue. The glue smells like fermented, green olive juice. I love green olives. Well, I did until my face died on my ear. Now the smell makes me gag, similar to my reaction to pelicans. Slather yourself in science experiment stench and see if you can stomach an olive afterward. Bet not.

I was supposed to live with that stink for three weeks, but my ear and everything around it exploded on day three, which is why Doc and I are in crisis mode early on a Sunday morning. The glue applied to my body caused a rash response like poison ivy. My tuba-shaped ear is leaking toxins. Picture a water balloon poked plum full of pin pricks with fluid spraying through the tiny holes, running down your neck, back, and shoulder.

Doc slathers my inflamed parts with steroid cream, quickly plugs the leaks with new gauze, and tapes me up without glue. The gauze will degrade into a saturated diaper before lunch, so he tells me frequent changes are mandatory and will have to be kept up for days. I must look like I'm drowning in defeat, because I am. Doc digs deep for a positive spin on a rotten situation and says, "This is a hurdle, not a dead end. The flap is still alive."

When a transplant is completely unattached, it's called a skin graft. When it's still attached, it's a flap. For better blood supply, my transplant is attached as a flap. Deep within the slop swamping my head, the flap is still alive. I must ride out the allergic reaction flooding my ear while also keeping the flap afloat.

There's a lot of dripping involved. It's disgusting. Changing gauze twice a day turns into six times a day. I have so much absorption taped to my head, I look like I'm stuck to a maxi pad. And every time I change dressings, I have to lay the top half of my body over the bathroom sink to catch the sun-tea colored streams coming out of my ear. My body really doesn't like green olive goo. It's spitting it out something fierce. I've never touched poison ivy, and by all the juice that is running from my highest point, I desperately hope I never do. It's painful and repulsive.

The drainage is the consistency of blood. Runny, but not cold, my life force oozing down my neck through my hair into my ear canal. I'm enduring torture by a tap of my own making because my skin cancer is my fault.

Sometimes I can hear a histamine reaction dripping directly into my ear canal, instead of running the curved outer ridge of it. It's maddening and impossible to ignore. Our brains respond when our bodies signal bleeding, so every few minutes I panic that I'm bleeding somewhere. It's an auto response with no off button. The sensation is similar to how a bloody nose feels. We instantly respond by plugging our nostrils. I leak every few minutes with the release coming from my ear instead of my nose.

When I ask my husband for help taping the back side, which I can't see in the mirror, he looks for one second, gags for ten seconds—an audible gag to be sure—and leaves the bathroom. I'm on my own with this yuck job, but I laugh like I haven't laughed in days. In sickness and in health really means in sickness and in hell. He said, "I do" two decades ago so I'm the weeping treasure he has to sleep with. Me and all the towels I stack around me to contain my trough of toxins as I excrete poison ivy by proxy for a week.

# SEX

MY EAR OOZE thickens to crust a week later. I peel away layers, like a sun burn, every time I change the dressing. The limitation on social gatherings during pandemic times carries additional weight for me these days. I couldn't go anywhere with this ordeal on my head, anyway. Doc can't go anywhere either. Our house is still COVID free, but he's in quarantine with his sick kids. I send him photos of my ear via texts, so he can monitor my progress. Modern medicine.

Crusting indicates a reduction in infection, but it's still putrid, so I change covers but never walk around exposed. There's no way I'm letting this putrid process out of its trappings for anyone to see on my bi-monthly trip to the grocery store—the only place I go lately. The pandemic still rages on, so going out is still relegated from date night to stocking the pantry.

I have one exciting afternoon out when an osprey is injured. It needs a ride to the animal hospital for a bleeding wing. I'm a certified Idaho Master Naturalist. That means I take classes to learn about wildlife and wild lands, and I volunteer to help both. That also means I'm on the emergency call list when a biologist finds an injured bird that needs a ride to the Teton Raptor Center over the hill from Idaho Falls in Jackson, Wyoming.

My instructions are simple. Turn the music down and the A/C up. They didn't mention anything about speeding, so I speed until I'm pulled over ten minutes away from my destination, where the limit drops from 55 mph to 35 mph. I didn't slow down, but I immediately fess up when the officer approaches my driver's side window.

"I'm speeding for a good reason," I say in a rush. "There's a wild bird in my back seat."

The officer looks over my front seat to the dog crate on my back seat. We both hear talons clicking on the plastic bottom of the crate like long fingernails thrumming on a counter, or the click-clack of high heels on the hard floors at a shopping mall.

"It's an injured osprey," I say without smiling. "I'm its ambulance and it's surprisingly hard not to speed with a wild bird at your back."

The law raises his eyebrows in surprise. I mean, who wouldn't? I'm a woman with a taped head driving a fish-wrapped truck that has a wild bird in the backseat. He asks for my license, but doesn't ask me to open the crate. Good thing because that's the other instruction I have to follow. Don't open the crate. The bird will want out. The person I'm meeting at the raptor center is a trained handler. She gets to open the crate, not me.

While I wait for the officer to check my records, I think about the osprey I'm transporting and the one I was recording a few months ago. That one was using its talons to hold on to its meal, a fish at Bonneville Dam. It was helping itself to dinner at the beginning of this journey. Now I'm helping the same kind of bird at the end of this journey, but this osprey is in Idaho, not Oregon, so it eats trout instead of salmon.

The cop comes back to my truck with my license but not a ticket. My do-good deed, helping an osprey, is to my benefit. He sends me on my way with a warning.

Other than that quick out and back for a raptor rescue, I'm in. I worry that I'm liking my time inside too much. After three months on the couch growing bone and now another stay-in for a global virus plus ear and chest surgeries, I'm concerned about my outdoor desires. But it's not just germs keeping me in. Masks are too. They're painful on my ear mid-process on rebuild.

When my older son forgot his mask, he grabbed mine so he could go into the salon for his haircut appointment. I always keep two masks in my truck. As he exited the passenger side, I said, "Sharing masks is like sharing underwear."

He laughed as he retreated, but when he returned with his unkempt pandemic hair trimmed to order, he wasn't laughing.

"I'm not borrowing your mask ever again," he'd hotly said.

"Good," I told him. "You don't wear my underwear, so don't wear my mask."

"It's not that," he replied. "It's your make-up. It's all over the straps."

I laughed, laughed, laughed, and laughed some more while he stared at me confused.

"Silly boy," I said wiping giggle drops from my eyes. "When have you ever seen me wear that much make-up? That's not make-up. That's ear blood. Every time I snap a mask strap on my stitched ear, it bleeds. That's old blood snugging up on your face."

He was appalled. Sharing ceased permanently.

The less I mask, the less I bleed so the less I roam among others, the less I have to masquerade. Snapping that elastic strap on a damaged ear feels like a whip across the softest skin on my backside. I'm not a nice shopper having an afternoon out after that snap. I'm pissed. I'm a pandemic shopper with a broken mask holder on the side of my head. I'm irritated and in pain and the guy on aisle five, with two perfectly shaped lobes that are wasting away as strap holders on his maskless face, could get an earful from me so it's best if I keep my distance. Better yet, others should keep away from the store. Especially the guy on aisle five.

Here's a plus. Doc didn't shave the hair on the left side of my head. But after countless rounds of taping and retaping, I've pulled out half of my hair one clump at a time. I don't think it feels dog-belly-rubbing good anymore.

When I'm not pounding on a keyboard to keep my hands out of my ear, I'm staring at my phone. It reminds me of listening for a dial tone on the kitchen telephone when I was a teenager. If it wasn't ringing, it wasn't working. Simple logic but flawed. There was always a tone, just not always a ring. Well, now I look at my phone instead of listening to it. Why doesn't the screen light up? Is it off? Is it broken? It's neither. There's nothing going on, so there's no reason for the screen to light up. Maybe my ringer is muted? No.

I wouldn't last long-term on call. I'm wound as tight as a corset when I'm on call. Just ring already! I mean *beep*. Let's go. I'm on call for salmon sex. Yes, salmon sex. Tuba-sized ears that spit sour juice don't foster affection, so I'm not having sex, but the salmon should be. They're late. Unlace that corset.

I finally receive word of frisky fish in early September. The text from Lytle lights up my morning. The Shoshone-Bannock keep researchers stationed in the narrow canyon cut by the Yankee Fork. Those researchers notify Lytle and Lytle notifies me, but only if there's action. There hasn't been any movement for weeks, not even after resetting my phone, so it feels like Christmas morning when Lytle pings me via text. Spawn on.

His crew walks the watershed daily, looking for redds. Redds are spots in the gravel bottom of a river, where fish have cleared an area to lay eggs. Once you know how to identify scoured river bottom, redds can be found. The tribe has found redds. It's like a grid switch. Salmon sex turns on that quickly, then disappears. Power on. Power off. A blink in the big scheme, and then it's gone. I'm searching for that blink.

Lytle's text means I have a shot at the blink, but the amorous appetites arrived three weeks late. This has me in fits. The Chinook were supposed to spawn in August. That's the historic deal. I scheduled my personal repairs around salmon sex in summer, not fall, but the fish waited for the leaves to turn this year. Salmon are laying future life in the Yankee Fork in September instead of August. That means I'm shooting mile 850 with stitches in four places. Four! It's unbelievable, but here I go. These fish don't quit, so neither do I.

When the "spawn on" text pops on my screen, I pop off the couch and start packing gear. I have a six-hour round-trip drive for a two-hour shoot and during those two hours, I must be delicate with myself and the fish. No ripping stitches and no touching redds.

Historically, an estimated three thousand Chinook used to return to the Yank. In 2020, thirty-seven precious and protected Chinook salmon made it all the way from the ocean to Idaho. They're at the final mile, mile 850, mustering enough energy for their final act. This is it. The "spawn" is the scientific term for mating fish, but I prefer my term: salmon sex.

Hotness loads my camera equipment into my rig with his stern, serious face.

"No lifting. No running. No falling," he says, reminding me that I'm temporarily fragile. "Be back here before dark, so we know you're safe."

I promise to use one piece of equipment at a time when I reach the river. I promise to be conservative with my shots, but I will have shots no matter what. Move slowly. Concentrate. Be careful. There's no room for error for me or the fish. Back on the migration route I go. I'll see the fish I've been following for 850 miles soon. Salmon die after they have sex. It's a one and done deal at the end of their journey. This is the one and the only funeral I've ever looked forward to.

# GRAVES

A SEATBELT SECURING a stitched chest for an extended drive doesn't sit well at all, but I tuck in tight and make it to the Yankee Fork before noon. Now I must find the fish and record their mating ritual before they die. I want to hurry, but both doctors forbid exercise. I'm not running twenty trail miles. I'm not even sweating. I'm barely moving. A slow stroll along the banks to look for spawning beds is not exercise. I won't bleed out. That's what I keep telling myself as I pace in waders.

I find a dead drifter first. I panic, thinking I'm too late. The Fork is full of dead fish. No headstones, no reaper, just graves. Shallow and uncovered graves, the decay of a marvelous migration complete with corpses. Adult spawners only last a day or two once they lay their eggs, and they'll stand guard until the permanent end. They won't willingly leave despite their zombie status, but eventually the current's pull is stronger than their ability to stay, and they're swept downstream. That's what I'm looking at. A spawned and spent sweeper. With the deed done, death comes.

I think past panic for sensible reason: I know a redd is close if I've seen a carcass. In the 1960s, there were four hundred redds in the Yankee Fork. This year there are twelve. Not even a baker's dozen, but I'm near one. Each redd needs two fish, one male and one female. If one is out, the other might still be in. And it will be standing guard. Keep pacing. Search the edges. Stay calm. I have stitches on my face, ear, scalp, and chest. I am a mess. Don't mess that up or this. Fish care nothing about my condition, but their condition means everything to me.

When I finally see the life I'm looking for, my eyes flood. I thought the first thing I'd do was roll tape, but I don't. I cry. The moment deserves reverence, so I don't hit the red record button yet. Instead, I watch a three-foot, sloth-speed slither weave in water so shallow that the salmon's back and body are exposed. The nearly non-existent sight blurs behind tears. I'm hooked. The fish has me. I don't move. I don't speak. I don't hesitate to record with my mind before I have to document with mechanics.

I'm looking at a fish that swam 850 miles through unbelievably terrible odds. An unpredictable flashback jolts me where I stand. Iceland. The last time I was this close to a salmon, without a window between us, was in Iceland in the fall of 2017.

In my memory, I'm situated on a bump of grass rooting its way into the Fljótaá River in Iceland's North Region. My earthen perch was barely bigger than my felt-soled wading boots, so my balance was precarious. Despite wobbling, I was content concentrating on the current in front of me. I didn't have to worry about snags on my back cast because there are no trees in Iceland. There's no shade either, but it was the island's first cold snap, so I welcomed the sun seeping over the top of surrounding ridges dusted white overnight after the northern lights went to bed.

"I think this is the most beautiful river in the whole world," said Gunnlaugur Gudleifsson, fly fishing guide and my new-found friend on foreign soil.

I almost agreed. Replace the sheep with cows and this could almost pass for some of my favorite fishing holes in Idaho. You'd have to swap fish too, sea trout for browns and Atlantic salmon for Pacific. I'd never caught a salmon. Ten minutes into my river rhythm, that changed.

"Wait for it. Let it run," Gunnlaugur said. "It will roll over and quit when it's done."

I nearly nosedived off my small grassy knoll when an Atlantic salmon ran with my fly in its jaw. I'm left-handed, but I fished with a rented rod. It was set up for a right-hander, so my fingers stumbled at first, but I recovered quickly enough. The set was solid. I stayed upright. The fish and I stayed connected. The feel of my first salmon was remarkable.

Most of the salmon species are so rare where I live, you can't catch them let alone keep them. When I explained the significance of the moment to Gunnlaugur he immediately understood and hollered, "Mariu Lax!" He was referring to the Mary salmon, or virgin fish. This was my first salmon, my virgin fish.

By Icelandic tradition, you kill your first salmon and eat its adipose fin with a shot of Brennivín, an island alcohol that tastes like a cross between vodka and Jäger.

"I would prefer the shot," Gunnlaugur said. "The fin is just jelly. It doesn't really taste like anything."

The fin-eating part of the tradition has fallen to the wayside, but not because it lacks taste. Tradition is changing because the fishery's caretakers are changing.

"Iceland people are opening their eyes to nature," said Höddi Birgir, the other fly angler I met in Iceland. He's younger, taller, and bossier than Gunnlaugur. "And I'm one of the guys building up the river."

Höddi started practicing catch and release almost two decades ago on the North Region's Húsey River. At first, the farmers he rents river from couldn't swallow the idea of catching something they couldn't eat. In Iceland, fish are for supper, not for sport. Fish are eaten multiple times daily. They don't put perfectly edible fish back in the water. Höddi didn't either until the year he counted seventeen Atlantic salmon in the Húsey.

"Past days of seventeen is ridiculous. It's almost nothing," he said. "My brothers and I probably hooked ten of those seventeen. That was the year I knew we needed to make a change."

The change is significant but still unfamiliar to Icelandic people. When Höddi and I walked into a local café wearing waders, the waiter thought we were rafters. Rafting in waders is suicide. Trying to explain that to people who would rather sit in hot pools than stand in cold water is frustrating. Figuring out Iceland's fly fishing formula is just as frustrating.

Public fishing is not the norm in Iceland like it is in the US. Höddi pays farmers for access to beats, sections of river. Farmers own the fish swimming in current, crossing their fields. Höddi keeps track of how many fish his angling customers catch and release in every farmer's beat. Höddi counted 370 salmon in the Húsey in 2016. Catch rates go up as release rates gain favor. Release rates gain favor because farmers are paid more for productive pools. Thousands more. The river is giving them something.

It gave me something too. I caught a sea trout on the Húsey and then, an Atlantic salmon on the Fljótaá. My first salmon. My virgin. The salmon was twenty-five inches of ocean wild, and it left my hand just as fast as it took my fly.

"There's a bigger one underneath that one," Gunnlaugur said. "I try to catch him, but he just pushes the fly out of the way."

From where we stood, I could see the salmon's complete lifecycle. You're never far from ocean when you're on an island. There were maybe two dozen miles between freshwater and saltwater where we were. I was standing where the salmon was born. I could see where it grew up and where it would die. I saw all of that from where I was standing in Iceland. I don't see all three parts of a salmon's lifecycle when I'm standing in Idaho. Probably one, maybe two of those milestones, but definitely not three.

I see the birthplace, and I know the growing up phase plays out 850 miles away. I can also see the grave, but most Idaho-bound fish won't see their nature-designated grave. They'll die in some unexpected way in some unplanned plot before they make it to their intended graves.

I don't want Iceland. I want Idaho. I file the unique island visit and refresh my mind with the familiar state I live in, the place where I stand now. I'm near the spawn spot, watching a fish that found its intended grave. It's one of only thirty-seven fish that made it to the finish line. Thirty-seven. That's it. And of those thirty-seven, at least twenty-four got lucky. Each of the twelve redds house about three thousand fertilized eggs. Those eggs will winter on the Yank, flush to the ocean for two to three years, then return to their cribs as adults just like their parents did. That's the intention, but the pretty turns ugly.

What's left of Idaho's prime habitat could host 127,000 salmon. The endangered species threshold is 31,750 salmon. In 2020, 8,565 wild spring Chinook salmon crossed Lower Granite Dam. Thirty-seven of those made it to the Yank to lay eggs. Of the several thousand eggs incubating, only a few dozen will make it back to spawn and die in their home water.

Females tend to build the bed and stand guard more often, so I assume I'm looking at a lady. She's drop-dead beautiful. Her nose and fins are white with rot, and there's a large, gouged-out hole on her bottom half. Is that where her eggs once rode? There are scratches and nips on her top half. Eagle talons or osprey beaks? Her wounds are as puzzling as my own, but she's still beautiful. Beautiful in Mother Nature's eyes and in mine. I see her.

I see her even though she doesn't see me. I acknowledge her rare existence, her importance. I recognize the risk she took to get here. I recognize my own risk to get here. I know she's exhausted. I'm exhausted. But there's nowhere else she should be, and nowhere else I should be. She's doing her thing for fish of the future until her own clock stops, and I have the privilege of witnessing the marvel of her last mile.

You can tell she's putting every last bit of her energy into the gravel. It's astounding. It's humbling. Every few minutes, she lets her guard down and the current carries her away. Like a pulse, there's a rhythm to it. I count the beats. She returns, she guards, she lets go again. That's my cue. Two steps and I'm in the flow. I keep my feet and camera away from her redd, and angle my lens, so it will look directly at her when she comes back. My camera is smaller than my hand and wrapped with webbing around a flat, smooth rock the size of a dinner plate. The whole contraption is pitched underwater on the river bottom upstream from the action and well out of the hot zone. Her bed is not my bed to hop into, so I make sure I don't.

The rock adds weight holding the lens securely in place in swift, shin-deep water. It's always surprising when you realize such large fish choose such small water, but it's to my documenting benefit. Depth adds darkness. There may be important secrets way down there in the dark, but that's not where the fish I want to see go, and if they did go there, I wouldn't see them. My lens wouldn't either. Natural light doesn't reach deep, and neither do I. On these shoots, I pack waders but never scuba gear because the best shots aren't deep. I've never worn scuba gear or breathed with a tank and hose, though viewers might think I have when looking at some of my shots. Water is deceptive like that, throwing off perceptions.

Natural light filtering in from above the surface makes shallow shots more appealing. Sure, I now know how to put my head underwater, but I don't need to. Most of my underwater shots are done by dropping a camera under and leaving it alone while the fish come around. They're unaware that I'm near, but sometimes they're curious about the tiny, shiny, silver square with a red blinker set in record mode. From underneath by lens, salmon look fully saturated, but from the bank by naked eye, I can see that their backs are out of the water.

I wonder if salmon know when they're in half bath with some of their parts out. Is there a draft? Different acoustics? Increased anxiety? I know when I'm half-bath, I endure all three and I don't like any of it. Half-bath is high risk. No wonder talons and beaks take stabs at salmon. They're exposed in half-bath. I feel exposed in half-bath, too, my wounds out of the water. My disappointment drowning in desperation.

But for filming, shallow is in my favor. It promotes ideal lighting conditions if I can secure the camera in the current, so it doesn't shake. That's what the rock is for. I test it by wiggling the rock cam. It doesn't budge; it will hold. I push record, take two steps out, and I'm back on the bank before the next beat.

I hide my shadow in the willows and wait for her return. It doesn't take long. She's so tired of going against the current, but she hates to be away. She has to get back until there's no going back.

She's moving, but I'm motionless. She swims over her redd and stops. I peek over the bushes and freeze. She hovers with strength the swimming dead shouldn't have. I squeeze my hands together with silent delight I didn't expect. She shimmies. I shiver. She noses a few pea-sized stones, then settles in guard mode. I settle in to watch her hold until the pull wins again, and she drifts away to start the dance again. Till death does she part.

I finally have the last act at the last mile. I'll add it to the rest of the shots I've collected from the ocean to Idaho over the last four months. I have twenty-five hours of footage to shove into a twenty-six-minute show. It's like shoving stepsister's foot into Cinderella's slipper. It's an impossible fit, but this whole journey proved impossible, yet here we are. She and I. Both of us falling apart. One of us drifting away. The other fading away. Which one is which, I'm not sure. The distinction isn't sharp.

I knew this migration had a morbid end, but it's soul-rattling, nonetheless. It proves to me we're off, way off. We need to let the wild be wild. We know nothing of what interrupting nature means for our own existence. If we did, we would choose otherwise, and we would choose in unison. No arguing. No resistance. Just righting our wrongs because letting the wild be wild will be this planet's saving grace and ours.

# RIBBONS

I WORE RAINBOWS of ribbon as a little girl. Ribbons in my hair for every dance recital. Ribbons around my neck kept my house key close. Ribbons pinned on my shirt at the end of another soccer season, another spelling bee, another school year.

All of those childhood ribbons matter. They're what ribbons should be at a young age, important and tangible. My boys have ribbons, trophies, and medals. Each one matters to them, and I recognize that. That's why the shelf of honor in each of their bedrooms is so dusty. I don't touch their shrines, not even to swipe dust away. I look at them when I'm collecting clothes off the floor on laundry day, but I don't touch them. I like that I still recognize what holds value to children. What matters to my kids matters to me. I get it. I didn't want my mom moving my ribbons when I was little either.

I bet Maddy wears ribbons. She's a fifth grader at Donnelly Elementary School near McCall, Idaho. She's raising fish in class. The salmon eggs are in tanks wrapped in black construction paper. The Nez Perce Tribe collected the eggs from Chinook passing Lower Granite Dam and entrusted them with Mrs. Abrams class. She's the kind of all-in, hands-on creative teacher so many of us learn the most from because she's interactive, involved.

We have a screen visit when I have a signal. I show the kids what I'm seeing on the road. They show me the one shot I'll never collect in the wild: the heartbeat of a hatching salmon egg. It's an alevin, the lifecycle phase that consists of a tiny tail with a spine, eyes, and a yolk sack. This is status quo before a fish is considered fry and can swim around looking for other things to eat once its own feed sack is gone. Fish are translucent in alevin stage, so the blood red heart, and its pulsing beat, are visible in a clear tank with clean gravel and calm water. That visibility isn't possible out in the elements, but it's cool to see in a classroom. Even cooler to hear kids explain their observations, documenting behavior most adults would never notice.

Maddy is eleven, and she's first to speak when I stop talking. She approaches the front of the room toward the computer cam. She's masked. The whole class is masked, but only half of the class is there. The other half have to watch a recorded version of me later. A full class won't happen during a pandemic, but half class is better than no class, so we work with what we've been dealt.

When Maddy is closer to me on screen than she is to the other kids in class, she pushes her light blue mask below her chin so I can see her full face and hear her voice unobstructed. The mask-down gesture is commonplace after this many months. Screen-face is commonplace too. It's how children are learning while we're living at a safe social distance. Screen time is as normal to Maddy as a chalkboard was half a century ago, no eraser dust needed. She knows to talk to me like I'm physically there, even though I'm not.

We're both curious by nature and casual in conversation, so the banter starts easily enough. I notice that we look alike. She probably doesn't think so, but I do. Her straight brown hair is gathered in one ponytail at the back of her head. I wore my hair the same way at her age, unless I branched out with one ponytail on either side of my head above my ears with the part always crooked, so one pony hung heavier than the other. Old class pictures still remind me of my shy, cockeyed days. My favorite shirt when I was her age read, "Kid for Rent." Her shirt reads, "I am the future." I like her shirt better.

The tanks wrapped in black paper are at the back of the classroom. She points to them in the background and tells me salmon get scared. She knows they're scared by how they eat.

"Trout will swim to the top when you feed them, but salmon won't," Maddy says. "They sit on the bottom and wait for food to fall. They won't come up 'cause they're scared."

Black paper blocks scary stuff. The less salmon see, the more relaxed they are. That's why the tanks are covered. Unlike me when I was little and afraid of the dark, young salmon do better in the dark. They're hiding. I hid by avoiding eye contact. Salmon hide by avoiding all contact. It's dark down in the gravel at the bottom of the river, even in shallow spawning beds. Hide, stay alive. There's a lot of scary stuff to come when you're older. Don't look at it when you first hatch. It's too scary. Makes sense to me now that Maddy has made sense of it for me. Never underestimate the generation that's in your shadow, the one that's learning by your example, be it hidden or on display.

Her ponytail isn't bedazzled. No ribbons this late in the school day, but maybe there were when she arrived, and they're shoved in her backpack for the return home. I don't have ribbons in my hair either, not the kind you're picturing, anyway. The ribbons of adulthood are different. They're still important but not as literal, at least not by traditional definition.

The ribbons I wear as an adult are not the ribbons I wore as a young ballerina. Now my ribbons are brown mud instead of pink satin. Ribbons of water run down my legs when I pedal wet mountain trails and paddle the rivers running through those mountains. From the air, those rivers look like ribbons. I love those ribbons. They are life in liquid form. Like veins pumping blood through our bodies with vitality, rivers are our planet's vitality and the fish within, its heartbeat.

Before I was twenty, I knew fish as food. I knew we ate them, and I knew we raised them, different fish for each purpose. For eating, my cousins taught me how to gut trout at family reunions when we camped by stocked ponds. Foil, butter, and fire before eating. For raising, my brother had a bowl in his bedroom. Sometimes it hosted goldfish from the school carnival. Other times, he had two separate bowls, each housing a betta fish because if bettas share a bowl, they'll kill each other. I also knew other people raised fish because I saw them at hatcheries, threw pellets at them thinking I was feeding them so later they'd feed me. The fish my family ate and raised were always in water, but I never saw them in river water.

After I turned twenty, that changed. Mountains dominated my view growing up in Salt Lake City, whereas river dominated my view when I signed my first TV news reporting contract, sending me to Idaho Falls in my mid-twenties. That's when I realized fish don't just live in water. They live in rivers. Ribbons. I learned to catch fish with a fly, eat some, and put some back. I covered stories about stocking programs. I clipped fins of hatchery trout in raceways, then followed those hatchery trout to easy-access urban ponds and hard-to-reach high-mountain lakes to be stocked for someone else to catch. Fish stories—the fluffy feature kind and the hard news issue kind—seemed limitless. More limitless than the actual subject of those stories.

As the years add up, I keep fewer and fewer fish, and I catch fewer and fewer fish yet I still fish. In my forties, I have extra waders to share with everyone, more flies than I'll ever be able to fling in my lifetime, and more fly rods than casting arms.

A four-piece fly rod traveled the whole migration route with me. It only came out of its case in the camper once and I caught zero fish. It was the end of a shooting day on the Salmon River near Challis, Idaho. Bighorn sheep were on the opposite bank, a bald eagle downstream, and a cattle ranch upstream. The rock face across from me looked like sunset—pale by the river's edge, fading up to orange creamsicle in the center, and marbling to hot-poker red at the top. Its reflection late in the day turned the surface of the Salmon River the color of hot coals in the bottom of a campfire. I had to connect with it.

I was done shooting footage, and I was two hours ahead of schedule. With chores done, I granted myself an hour of fun. The setting felt ripe so I fished. I say I fished, but really what I did was connect. I still like to fish, but I'm beginning to think I like spending time where fish live more. I'm realizing my place among fish is really my place in the river.

I pulled the top half of my waders, bunched at my belted waist, up my trunk and clipped the straps over my shoulders. I waded into the river, stopping hip-deep, rod in my left hand. I watched my cast unroll over my head. I watched the fly land on the water. I watched the river move my fly for too long, so long that drag created such a wake behind the fly that I wouldn't fool a fish with it, and yet I stayed. I stayed connected to the river without connecting hook with fish. I wanted to be with them without touching, hooking, or taking them. I wanted to be in their river, to wear their ribbons.

Try it. Connect with those ribbons in any way you can. You don't need fancy equipment, swimming lessons or a rafting permit. Just stick your feet in a creek. That counts. Connect with this world that we rely on yet so often ignore. It is sincerely true, we need this planet more than it needs us. Touch what sustains you. Let moving water move you. See it for what it is, a worthy ribbon with prominent position in your shrine.

We all have the honor of wearing river ribbons on our legs, and in our hair, when we fish, float, swim, and soak. Recreate in our rivers and respect our rivers, but most of all, let salmon swim our rivers. If their swim means our sacrifice, I'm in. Everyone will have to give up something if we expect these disappearing fish to gain anything.

We stand to lose what we're used to. We will have to make adjustments. We'll have to change and change is scary. Black paper won't hide what has to happen, the unknotting of the ribbons. Letting them loose. Saving fish and saving farms takes cooperation, adaptation, and genius. We expected these things when the dams went in. We must demand them if the dams blow out, but never shall the ribbons shred.

So much interferes with salmon migration from the Oregon coast to the Idaho wilderness. It's hard to believe any fish survive the journey with all of us weighing heavy on the watershed with our own wants, but some do. And now, we've all seen what it takes to live life for one reason. To swim for future's sake from the ocean to Idaho.

May we all wear ribbons.

# AUTHOR'S ADVICE

"Work for it rather than wish for it."
—Kris Millgate